T0326558

SDR: from Bretton Woods to a world currency

P.I.E. Peter Lang

Bruxelles · Bern · Berlin · New York · Oxford · Wien

Elena FLOR

SDR: from Bretton Woods to a world currency

Federalism
Vol. 11

This book is jointly published by the *Robert Triffin International* (www.triffininternational.eu) and the *Centro Studi sul Federalismo* (www.csfederalismo.it).

Library of Congress Cataloging-in-Publication Data

Names: Flor, Elena, author.
Title: SDR : from Bretton Woods to a world currency / Elena Flor.
Description: New York : P.I.E. Peter Lang, [2019] | Series: Federalism ; 11 |
   Includes bibliographical references and index.
Identifiers: LCCN 2018054889| ISBN 9782807610170 (print : alk. paper) | ISBN
   9782807610187 (epdf) | ISBN 9782807610194 (epub) | ISBN 9782807610200
   (mobi)
Subjects: LCSH: Special drawing rights. | United Nations Monetary and
   Financial Conference (1944 : Bretton Woods, N.H.) | Money. | International
   finance.
Classification: LCC HG3898 .F57 2019 | DDC 332.4/5--dc23 LC record available at
   https://lccn.loc.gov/2018054889

This publication has been peer reviewed.

© P.I.E. PETER LANG S.A.
   International Academic Publishers
   Brussels, 2019
   1 avenue Maurice, B-1050 Brussels, Belgium
   brussels@peterlang.com; www.peterlang.com

Printed in Germany

ISSN 2294-6969
ISBN 978-2-8076-1017-0
ePDF 978-2-8076-1018-7
ePUB 978-2-8076-1019-4
MOBI 978-2-8076-1020-0
DOI 10.3726/b15076
D/2018/5678/103

Bibliographic information published by "Die Deutsche Nationalbibliothek".
"Die Deutsche National Bibliothek" lists this publication in the "Deutsche Nationalbibliografie"; detailed bibliographic data is available on the Internet at <http://dnb.de>.

Table of Contents

CHAPTER 1

The Bretton Woods Conference (1944)

At the 1892 International Monetary Conference in Brussels, convened by the United States, German economist Julius Wolf put forward a new solution to the problem of international payments: deposit a gold reserve in a neutral country and *issue international banknotes* based on it.[1] The problem addressed by Wolf was related to creating sufficient international liquidity to foster the development of economies and trade.

The gold standard, despite having facilitated the extraordinary development of international trade in the century between the end of the Napoleonic Wars and the outbreak of the First World War (the *Pax Britannica* period), ended up curbing economic development due to a gold shortage and its uneven distribution throughout the world. Gold, which was useful in creating relations among sovereign states, ultimately regulated by the war, was dismissed by John Maynard Keynes as a "barbarous relic". On the other hand, systems based on notes and coins could only be created if they were founded on trust, hence within empires and national states that ensured compliance with the laws underpinning the markets. A commodity, gold, was a real guarantee of the first system,[2] while trust in banknotes lays in the purchasing power of any goods or services and in the power to discharge financial obligations, as they were recognised throughout the national territory.

An idea similar to Wolf's was proposed in 1944, two world wars later, by John Maynard Keynes, British plenipotentiary at the International Monetary Conference of Bretton Woods. He illustrated the aims of his project as follows:

> We need an instrument of international currency having general acceptability between nations, so that blocked balances and bilateral clearings are unnecessary... We need an orderly and agreed method of determining the relative exchange values of national currency units, so that unilateral action

---

[1] Joseph Alois Schumpeter, *History of Economic Analysis*, London, Allen & Unwin, 1954 (Italian translation, *Storia dell'analisi economica*, Turin, 1959, p. 1319).

[2] The coexistence of gold and silver in bimetallic systems was unstable and short-lived.

and competitive exchange depreciations are prevented. We need a *quantum* of international currency, which is neither determined in an unpredictable and irrelevant manner as, for example, by the technical progress of the gold industry, nor subject to large variations depending on the gold reserve policies of individual countries; but is governed by the actual current requirements of world commerce and is also capable of deliberate expansion and contraction to offset deflationary and inflationary tendencies in effective world demand. We need a system possessed of an internal stabilising mechanism, by which pressure is exercised on any country whose balance of payments with the rest of the world is departing from equilibrium in either direction, so as to prevent movements which must create for its neighbours an equal but opposite want of balance. We need an agreed plan for starting off every country after the war with a stock of reserves appropriate to its importance in world commerce, so that without undue anxiety it can set its house in order during the transitional period to full peace-time conditions. We need a central institution, of a purely technical and non-political character, to aid and support other international institutions concerned with the planning and regulation of the world's economic life. More generally, we need a means of reassurance to a troubled world, by which any country whose own affairs are conducted with due prudence, is relieved of anxiety for causes which are not of its own making, concerning its ability to meet its international liabilities; and which will, therefore, make unnecessary those methods of restriction and discrimination which countries have adopted hitherto, not on their merits but as measures of self-protection from disruptive outside forces.[3]

This declaration of intent described the needs that the international monetary system should meet to be sufficiently fair, symmetrical, cooperative, sustainable and conducive to economic development; conditions that are still lacking in the current "non-system".

The "Keynes Plan" envisaged the creation of a clearing union and a reserve unit, the *bancor*. The union was based on the principle of central banks: it was to be a world central bank, use a unit of account issued by itself, record credits and debits in *bancor* of the nations, respective to their favourable or unfavourable balances of payments, and ensure major future developments. "Keynes certainly had in his mind that, if international plans for investment, commodity stabilisation, etc., were developed the Union would be able to help... A World Central Bank would be in an extremely powerful position owing to its ability to create credit".[4]

---

[3]   The excerpt is quoted in Roy Forbes Harrod, *The Life of John Maynard Keynes*, London, Macmillan, 1951, pp. 526-527.

[4]   R.F. Harrod, *op. cit.*, p. 550.

At Bretton Woods the "White Plan"[5] was adopted rather than the "Keynes Plan". The US dollar, rather than the *bancor*, was to function as the international currency and could be converted into gold at a fixed price of $35 per ounce (dollar-exchange standard). A supranational institution was not to govern the international currency, but the US Federal Reserve (also referred to as the Fed). The regime of fixed exchange rates was to be offset by national controls on capital movements, i.e. by nationalising economic policies. The names of the "Bretton Woods Institutions" were those designated by Keynes, i.e. the World Fund and World Bank, but their functions were very different.

Faced with a Europe ravaged by wars, the United States became the centre of the world economy. The institutions designed for common management became the basis for a reconstruction led by the only power left in the field. Establishing the dollar as the international currency, the US veto right in the International Monetary Fund, the use of World Bank financing to promote a new international division of labour, the privilege attributed by the GATT rules to countries with larger markets, all became in fact instruments for a reconstruction that would facilitate the United States in its reconversion from a wartime to a peace-time economy and promote American exports, and constituted the backbone of the post-war economic system.

However, in the last lines of his *The General Theory* Keynes warned that: "The practical men who believe themselves to be quite exempt from any intellectual influence, are usually the slaves of some defunct economist. Madmen in authority, who hear voices in the air, are distilling their frenzy from some academic scribbler of a few years back… Sooner or later, it is ideas, not vested interests, which are dangerous for good or evil".[6] What is more, the idea of the *bancor* has – for the best – continued to move forward, awaiting the emergence of the historical conditions needed for its implementation: a less divided and unbalanced world, a

---

[5] Harry Dexter White (1892-1948) was the US negotiator who was opposed to Keynes at the Bretton Woods Conference.

For a detailed account of the Bretton Woods Conference, in addition to Keynes' biography by Harrod, *op. cit.*, see also Robert Skidelsky, *John Maynard Keynes. Fighting for Freedom, 1937-1946*, New York, Viking, 2000 – this is the third volume of Keynes' monumental biography – and Benn Steil, *The Battle of Bretton Woods. John Maynard Keynes, Harry Dexter White, and the Making of a New World Order*, Princeton University Press, 2013.

[6] John Maynard Keynes, *The General Theory of Employment, Interest and Money*, London, Macmillan, 1936.

more cooperative and advanced world in the transition from the law of force to the force of law.

The switchover from a national to a supranational currency began to be prepared, precisely within the Bretton Woods Institutions, thus trying to return to its original function.

One "dilemma" was quickly uncovered by one of the first economists to collaborate with the IMF, Robert Triffin. He denounced the "scandal" of an international monetary system that condemned poor countries to financing the rich ones, conceived the special drawing rights (SDRs) of the IMF, participated in the establishment of the European Payments Union (EPU) and collaborated with the European Commission on the path that led from the European Unit of Account (EUA) to the European Currency Unit (ECU) and finally to the euro.[7]

---

[7]   Robert Triffin (1911-1993). "Belge devenu américain; américain redevenu belge, Triffin fut un citoyen européen et un citoyen atlantique. Critique sévère de la politique monétaire des États-Unis quand il dénonçait le cynisme avec lequel Washington utilisait le système de Bretton Woods pour faire payer par ses partenaires le déficit américain, il fut aussi, avec talent et inventivité, l'économiste militant en faveur de la création d'une monnaie européenne", this is how Michel Dumoulin and Alexandre Lamfalussy recall him in the preface to Catherine Ferrant and Jean Sloover (eds.), *Robert Triffin, Conseiller de princes. Souvenirs et documents*, Bruxelles, Peter Lang, 2010. For an overview of Triffin's work see: Robert Triffin, *Dollaro, euro e moneta mondiale*, edited by Alfonso Iozzo and Alfred Steinherr, Bologna, 1998. It is an anthology, published on the initiative of Il Mulino and the Compagnia di San Paolo, which bears witness to Triffin's participation in the debate on the monetary system between the creation of the IMF and the end of Bretton Woods, in particular concerning his opposition to the return to gold (gold standard), advocated by Jacques Rueff (De Gaulle's Economic Advisor), along with Triffin's subsequent contributions in the different stages of European monetary unification. We recommend reading it to learn more about the thought of Triffin, one of the most brilliant architects of the two existing supranational currencies: special drawing rights on the IMF and the euro. Work on his fascinating biography is still underway, but the first volume has already been published on the initiative of the Robert Triffin International: Jérôme Wilson, *Robert Triffin – Milieux académiques et cénacles économiques et internationaux (1935-1951)*, Bruxelles, Éditions Versant Sud, 2015.

CHAPTER 2

Special Drawing Rights (Sdrs) and the End of the Bretton Woods System (1967-1981)

It is easy to understand why the dollar was adopted as the international currency when the United States was in surplus on its current account during the "golden years" (1946-1965). The Bretton Woods monetary system reorganised the "free world" on the promise of the dollar's convertibility into gold. The US, spared from war on its own territory, produced the majority of the world's goods, possessed almost all the gold reserves and was the only country capable of financing reconstruction and post-war economic recovery. They did so in an exemplary way due to the fact that reconstruction clearly coincided with US national interest, to its improved understanding of the economy after the first post-war mistakes[8] and, finally, maybe also due to the US's historic idealism.

Triffin foresaw two different scenarios that might arise after adopting the dollar as the international currency (the *Triffin dilemma*):

– with a surplus US balance of payments, the dollar would be scarce and the development of the world economy and trade would be affected, which is what happened with the 1950s dollar shortage;

– or, contrarily, a deficit in the US balance would result in a surplus of dollars, then inflation and finally distrust of the dollar itself, causing it to lose its appeal as the international currency. This was what happened with the 1970s dollar inflation. The Korean War, and above all the Vietnam War, were financed not by taxes but by printing money, which was contingent upon the dollar being

---

[8]   Regarding how relations were handled between the winners and losers in the war, the tragic experience of the reparations imposed on Germany after WWI was decisive. Keynes, who was opposed to them, resigned as the British representative in peace negotiations claiming they were absurd in a famous pamphlet that already reflected the entirety of his thought: John Maynard Keynes, *The Economic Consequences of the Peace*, New York, Harcourt, Brace and Howe, 1920.

accepted as the international currency, which thus kept the US from having to ask American citizens for sacrifices equal to their cost.[9]

During the 1960s, the US used many instruments, such as swaps, to prevent, reduce or delay converting the dollar into gold, taking great benefit of international cooperation. Among these instruments it is worth mentioning *Roosa* Bonds: bonds issued *in foreign currency* by the US so that they could be included in central banks' portfolios instead of gold.[10] For the first time, the US borrowed in the creditors' currencies, and not in its own.

After declaring that the dollar could no longer be converted into gold, the gold-exchange standard became, also formally, a dollar standard allowing the US to finance, using its own currency, a long line of deficit in its external balance. Jacques Rueff criticised this as being the "*deficit without tears*". Giscard d'Estaing decried this "*exorbitant privilege*". Guido Carli called the accumulation of petrodollars a "*paper pyramid*".

Moreover, where there are no gold or foreign exchange constraints, the monetary authority of the country issuing reserve currency is continually torn: between the economic needs of the country to which it belongs, and needs stemming from the international use of the currency.

The three legacies of this period of unrest leading up to the declaration of the dollar's inconvertibility were:

1) the dollar's conversion into gold at 35 $/oz. – according to the Rueff/De Gaulle doctrine – especially by the Banque de France and the Bank of Italy, which were still in part holders;
2) the beginning of the European path towards monetary independence from the US and;
3) the creation of special drawing rights by the IMF.

---

[9] One very influential book introducing Triffin's thinking to a wider audience was: Robert Triffin, *Our International Monetary System: Yesterday, Today and Tomorrow*, New York, Random House, 1968.

[10] These bonds, also expressed in Italian lira, were named after Under Secretary of the US Treasury Robert V. Roosa. On their function during the crisis, please see this interesting interpretation by: John H. Makin, "Swaps and Roosa Bonds as an Index of the Cost of Cooperation in the 'Crisis Zone'", in *The Quarterly Journal of Economics*, Harvard University Department of Economics, May 1971 ("Crisis zone" is defined here as a condition where pressure exists to convert dollars into gold).

These three solutions are not necessarily mutually exclusive; so far they have rather complemented one another, and are more relevant today than ever.

The first legacy, of gold's convertibility, is deeply rooted in cultures such as those of the Middle Eastern oil-producing countries, and its use may be traced back to a past when precautionary requests were made for real guarantees between partners who did not trust each other.

The second aimed at protecting regional markets from dramatic exchange rate fluctuations caused by the pegging of each national currency to the dollar and paved the way to a multi-currency international monetary system. The creation of regional monetary areas – starting with the euro – spread, in fact, to other areas dealing with the de-dollarisation process.

The third looks explicitly at the *bancor*, the financial problems of developing countries and the need for a peg currency that stabilises the emerging multi-currency system (currently consisting of three major currencies, i.e. the dollar, the euro and the renminbi, and other minor currencies such as the yen and the pound sterling). Here, what interests us is the third legacy regarding the first serious dollar crisis, without, however, neglecting its important connections with the other two.

According to the provisions of the 1944 IMF Statute (Article III, Section 3), in respect of currency requirements concerning their balance of payments, member countries had ordinary drawing rights that they could exercise by depositing national currency in the Fund against foreign currencies. Each country could repurchase its own currency by depositing foreign currency in the Fund. A country's borrowing position started when the availability of that country's currency in the Fund was more than 75 % of its quota, i.e. when the country started to use its gold tranche (equal to 25 % of its quota). On the other hand, the availability of national currency in the Fund of less than 75 % of the quota indicated a credit position and attributed the country with a super gold tranche, i.e. the right to acquire foreign currency, in excess of its gold quota, equal to the credit claimed. Each country could draw additional foreign currency using four credit tranches each equal to 25 % of its quota (Article V of the Statute).

The creation of *Special Drawing Rights* (SDRs) on the IMF was agreed in 1967 and became effective in 1969 ("*First Amendment*" to the Statute). It aimed to offer member countries' official reserves an initially complementary currency, which at the time was a substitute for both gold and the dollar. The conversion of dollars into gold by major central banks raised fears of insufficient expansion of the international economy, trade and finance: gold because it was hoarded and the dollar because it was unsafe.

While France asked for a new financial instrument in line with the gold reserves held by each country, other states, including Italy, proposed the creation of an independent international reserve unit, to be distributed according to quotas in the Fund. The US rejected the French proposal, as it had already lost a substantial part of its gold reserves, and also the creation of a new international reserve unit, fearing that it might compete with the dollar. Instead, they proposed the more general use of existing automatic drawing rights on the IMF: the gold tranche and the credit tranches.

In this highly contested field, Rinaldo Ossola,[11] the chairman of an ad hoc committee, and Robert Triffin, devised a solution that was accepted by the US after lengthy negotiations. The new *special drawing rights* responded to the US's request to use existing instruments, but broke the taboo of the creation of international liquidity by the Fund. In fact, these were international cash resources with full currency convertibility made available to the Fund's member countries by the IMF *in addition to* member's entitlements under the statutory provisions of 1944. The 1967 Agreement provided that SDRs would gradually become the main international liquidity instrument, replacing national currencies (hence, especially the dollar) in performing this function.

The four credit tranches were raised from 25 % to 36.25 % of each country's quota, thus increasing the total amount of loans obtainable from 100 % to 145 % of the individual quotas. Moreover, in order to cope with the growing need for international liquidity, the currency reserves available to the Fund were gradually increased by expanding the capital shares of individual members and using the GAB (General Arrangements to Borrow) agreements, real agreements of mutual credit decided by the "Group of Ten"[12] and brokered by the IMF, which integrated the numerous specific facilities and the swap transactions stipulated within Basel's Bank of International Settlements (BIS).[13]

---

[11] Rinaldo Ossola (1913-1990), who had served the Bank of Italy since 1938, after 1945 worked mainly to include Italy in international economic institutions. In the 1960s, he collaborated with Governor Guido Carli, supported the creation of an international fiat currency. In this field, Ossola was his right hand man, both as a creator of technical solutions and as a negotiator. He became Director General of the Bank of Italy (1975-76) and Minister for Foreign Trade (1976-79).

[12] The members of the "Group of Ten" were: Belgium, Canada, France, Germany, Japan, Italy, the Netherlands, the United Kingdom, the United States and Sweden.

[13] The Bank for International Settlements (BIS), based in Basel, was established in 1930 and its main mission is to foster cooperation among central banks (sixty, to date), which are also its shareholders.

In 1969, it was agreed that general measures, concerning all members' quotas, could be approved only by a double majority of 3/5 of members and 85 % of the votes, and no longer by the 80 % provided for at Bretton Woods, so as to maintain US veto rights.

In the 1969 Agreements, in addition to the creation of special drawing rights, a "*Second Amendment*" was envisaged,[14] which introduced significant changes to Art. IV of the Statute in particular. It was only approved by the Assembly in 1976 and it:

- legalised the system of floating exchange rates, while the Bretton Woods system had been based on fixed exchange rates, which could be changed only under special circumstances and by mutual agreement;
- allowed each country to adopt the exchange rate regime that was more in line with national currency policies;
- reduced the role of gold by decreeing the end of its official price; (consequently)
- eliminated all gold obligations associated with the Fund, including those of the gold tranche, renamed the reserve tranche, which were no longer to be paid in gold, but rather in currencies accepted by the IMF or SDRs;
- de-committed about a third of the Fund's gold reserves, allocating the capital gain accrued, from the market value and the book value (still at 35 $/oz.) to developing countries (those participating in the IMF, not those belonging to the Soviet bloc).

Initially, the value of the SDR – albeit not convertible into gold – was not defined as equal to one dollar, but, as proposed by France, to the *gold content of one dollar*. Following the 1971 and 1973 dollar devaluations against gold, the SDR's exchange rate was revalued by around 20 %. The SDR's valuation of 1.20[15] dollars was the last time this was based on the US currency; in 1974 the Assembly of the Fund, noting the growing

---

[14]   For a history of the SDR and in particular the negotiation of the second amendment see: Christopher Wilkie, *Special Drawing Rights. The First International Money*, Oxford University Press, New York, 2012.

[15]   One SDR was equal to one dollar, i.e. 0.028571 oz. or 0.88857 grammes of fine gold (as the gold price per troy ounce was $ 35, equivalent to 31.10 grammes). The value in gold has remained unchanged even after the two dollar devaluations (in December 1971, from 35 to 38 $/oz., and in February 1973, from 38 to 42.22 $/oz.) with the resulting SDR revaluations equal to $ 1.08571 and $ 1.206375.

spread of fluctuating exchange rates and the failure to restore the dollar's gold convertibility, decided to transform the SDR into a basket of currencies, consisting of the sixteen currencies of the member countries that between 1968-72 had participated in world exports of goods and services with quotas that were no less than one per cent. Each country was given a weight equal to its exports compared to the world total. The exchange rate considered for each currency was the one against the dollar on 28 June 1974, which was then converted into SDRs at $ 1.20. The IMF then calculated the value of the SDR based on the value of the component currencies, multiplied by their relative weights.

Therefore, we can consider this date, thirty years after Bretton Woods, as the start date of the de-dollarisation of the world economy. The series of transformations of the IMF, starting from the end of the dollar/gold link and the consequent increase in the oil price (which went up tenfold between 1973 and 1979), was completed (again in 1974) with the increase in the quotas of the oil-producing countries from 10 to 20 % and with the creation of the oil facility.

In 1981 the composition of the SDR basket was radically changed to include, instead of the sixteen currencies with exports of more than 1 % of the world total, only the currencies of the top five exporting countries: the dollar, the mark, the franc, the yen and the pound sterling.

The basket composition was then modified during each five-year review, scheduled to record changes in the weight of the economies. The table below shows the most important changes following the creation of the euro, which replaced the mark and franc in early 1999, and the inclusion of the renminbi, which became effective in 2016.

With the 2000 review, the criterion used to determine currency weighting was also changed: in addition to the importance of exports (which continued to have a 50 % value), there were also indicators of the share of the currency in other countries' currency reserves, in loans and bond issues (for the other 50 %). The new criterion had to ensure that the currency included in the basket was "freely usable", thus excluding the Chinese currency as long as it was state-controlled. These changes again favoured the US, which was exporting less and less but still benefitting from the disproportionate use of the dollar in world reserves and the financial market.

The first SDR allocations to IMF members, in proportion to their respective quotas, took place between 1970-76, totalling SDR 8.9 billion: a very modest sum compared to over SDR 200 billion in international liquidity in the mid-1970s. In 1976, fifty-three currencies were pegged to the dollar, thirteen to the French franc, twelve to the SDR and five to the pound sterling. Six European countries (Germany, Belgium, the Netherlands, Denmark, Sweden and Norway) participating in the "snake in the tunnel", signed a joint float agreement against the dollar.

The second SDR allocation occurred between 1979-81, after the second oil shock, which, while bringing the accumulated amount to 21.4 billion, was still insufficient.

In 1997, after the Asian crises, the IMF's Board of Governors proposed a new issue, but it failed to get a majority vote (American veto) until 2009.

It was only after the 2007 financial collapse and the 2009 G-20 Summit that two major SDR issues were approved: 33 billion to take into account the countries that had joined the IMF after 1981 (more than 20 % of the members, also following the dissolution of the Soviet bloc) and 250 billion to increase the members' SDR reserves and support the global economic system on the basis of estimated "long-term" needs.

Essentially, following the dollar's inconvertibility and skyrocketing oil prices,[16] many IMF countries wanted to organise themselves into monetary areas with floating exchange rates between different areas, but basically fixed within them. At this stage, the plan to create supranational paper currency could be carried out more quickly in the areas with greater economic and political cohesion than might be possible at the global level at that time, where the country exercising the veto right in the IMF tenaciously defended the privilege of its own currency. The European integration process was already well underway and Triffin himself became convinced – so much so that it changed the course of his life, as we shall see – that this phase of European monetary unification was necessary to pave the way to a more widespread use of SDRs instead of gold and national currencies. Before examining the various phases in European monetary system, up to the creation of the euro, we should also mention the reasons underlying the short-lived success and rapid decline of the private SDR market.

---

[16] The oil producing countries reacted to the dollar's inconvertibility by defending the value of crude oil in gold. They implemented a run-up in the crude oil price with respect to the gold price. After the creation of the euro, this was also considered a good reference to which to peg crude oil, which continues to be expressed in dollars, given that its relationship with gold, hoarded for speculative reasons, was often difficult to maintain. See: David Hammes and Wills Douglas, "Black Gold. The End of Bretton Woods and the Oil-Price Shocks of the 1970s", in *The Independent Review*, Vol. IX, No. 4, Spring 2005, and Valentina Tosolini, "Analysing Commodity Prices: Trend for Crude Oil and Wheat in US Dollars, Euro and SDR", *RTI-CSF Research Paper*, December 2016.

Composition of one SDR

Period	≣USD	▬DEM	❚❚FRF	• JPY	⊞GBP
1981/85	42%	19%	13%	13%	13%
1986/90	42%	19%	12%	15%	12%
1991/95	40%	21%	11%	17%	11%
1996/98	39%	21%	11%	18%	11%
	≣USD	▦EUR		• JPY	⊞GBP
1999/00	39%	DM 21%	FF 11%	18%	11%
		32%			
2001/05	45%	29%		15%	11%
2006/10	44%	34%		11%	11%
2011/15	41.9%	37.4%		9.4%	11.3%
	≣USD	▦EUR	▦CNY	• JPY	⊞GBP
2016/20	41.73%	30.93%	10.92%	8.33%	8.09%

Source: International Monetary Fund

CHAPTER 3

The First Short Life of the Market for SDR-Denominated Financial Instruments (1975-1985)[17]

There must be a market for any currency to be used as a global currency; this is what guarantees its liquidity and allows it to be used, not only in official reserves, but in private portfolios as well. A market for SDR-denominated financial instruments was opened in 1975. A few private banks began to accept deposits in SDRs and the first SDR-denominated loans were issued in the long-term capital market. These instruments looked appealing, during a period of instability marked by sharp dollar depreciations (1977-1978),[18] to those wishing to diversify and index their investment portfolios. However, the fact that there were many different currencies in the basket made it overly complex. In fact, once the basket was simplified by reducing the number of currencies from sixteen to five, SDR transactions increased sharply, particularly in 1981.

The first SDR-denominated *bonds* were issued in 1975. By 1981 there had already been thirteen issues, including bonds and certificates, for a total of about SDR 560 million. The issuers were two private companies and eleven public institutions. Since late 1981 there have been no more issues.

All SDR loan agreements contained safeguard clauses in the event that the IMF were to change the basket (five-year reviews) or completely abolish the use of SDRs. Some agreements even provided for the possibility that one or more currencies in the basket could become unavailable.

---

[17] Regarding the private SDR market we consulted: George Hoguet and Solomon Tadesse, "The Role of SDR-Denominated Securities in Official and Private Portfolios", in *BIS Paper* No. 58, October 2011; Dorothy Sobol, "The SDR in International Private Finance", in *FRBNY Quarterly Review*, Winter 1981/82; Research and Treasurer's Departments IMF, *The Role of the SDR in the International Monetary System*, (edited by Juanita Roushdy), IMF Occasional Paper, No. 51, March 1987.

[18] These times opponents of austerity policies often stress that the German word *Schuld* means both *debt* and *guilt*. However, it may be helpful to keep in mind that the English *sharp depreciation* can also be translated as fraudulent depreciation.

The market in SDR-denominated *Eurobonds* also developed between 1975 and 1981, with eight issues, six of which by Scandinavian issuers: this accounted for just 273 million dollars, less than 0.5 % of all Eurobonds floated over the same period.

Commercial paper in SDRs was not issued until 1981 and totalled about SDR 1.2 billion. This instrument is different from Eurobonds in that it has a shorter maturity and a floating rate. The issuers were two Italian state companies (ENEL and Ferrovie dello Stato), a French multinational (Pechiney Ugine Kuhlmann) and the Spanish State Railways (Renfe).

Two things were unique about the French issue: first, principal and interest could be repaid directly in SDRs to the creditor's account at predesignated banks, thus eliminating currency transaction costs. Instead, these types of loans were generally repaid in dollars at the SDR/US$ exchange rate on the due date. Second, until the French franc was included in the SDR basket, such loans could only be repaid if they had been official authorised, which at the time was required for transfers in foreign currency.

The market of *syndicated credits* in SDRs went from zero to about 1.2 billion in 1981 and then stabilised in the following year, compared to a total of 104.3 billion syndicated credits in all denominations that same year. Seven borrowers raised funds using this instrument: three sovereign borrowers (Sweden, the Ivory Coast and Ireland), two electric utilities (one in Venezuela, the other in Spain), a Mexican public financing agency and an African regional development bank.

The largest credit issue, whose borrower was the Kingdom of Sweden, was at the beginning of 1981. Although initially set at SDR 200 million, it was raised to 500 million due to favourable market conditions. All issuers offered spreads in line with those offered by comparable debtors in individual currencies (around 0.5 % over LIBOR for industrialised countries).

Commercial Banks Deposits in SDRs were first offered in London in 1975. By the end of 1978, about twenty banks had decided to carry out transactions in SDRs. However, until 1981 banks could only cover their positions in SDRs by using the forward foreign exchange market for each of the sixteen currencies included in the basket. Some currencies, however, were traded on the spot market, but did not benefit from a developed forward market. Therefore, only a few banks offered SDR-denominated deposits, often limiting the amount to 3-5 million dollars. They also hedged against unprotected risk by offering a lower interest rate than the one they could get using the individual currencies. They managed to overcome this problem by simplifying the basket to five currencies, all of which were actively traded on the short and long-term markets. Therefore, in 1981 there was a sharp increase in SDR deposits. Two commercial banks offered current accounts in SDRs and the banks participating in the Euroclear and Cedel clearing systems for Eurobonds were able to purchase SDR-denominated bonds by debiting these accounts held by the clearing systems. These accounts could also be used when loans and bonds were issued to settle both receipts and payments on them. By the end of the year, 40-50 banks were operating in SDRs and deposit volume peaked at 5-7 billion, net of interbank deposits. Starting in 1982 deposits also began to experience the same decline as other instruments: amounting to about 2.2 billion at the end of 1985.[19]

The first *certificate of deposit* (CD) in SDRs was issued by the Chemical Bank's London Branch in June 1980 for 50 million at a fixed-rate. Many SDR CDs were issued privately by banks at individual borrowers' requests. In early 1981, a group of seven banks in London announced that it would issue and trade certificates, ensuring them a secondary market. Several issues followed in the same year and brought the total to SDR 500-700 million. The minimum deposit for a certificate was SDR 1 million, far less than the 3-5 million usually required for term deposits. Interest rates were only slightly lower than those of deposits (about 1.8 %) because they were easy to trade. Starting in 1982, SDR CD interest rates also fell and trade volumes shrunk significantly.

A rather modest amount (SDR 55 million) of SDR CDs with longer maturity and a floating rate (2-3 years against 2-3 months) were issued in 1981 by Kuwaiti and Japanese banks.

In 1981 a modest forward market of SDR-denominated instruments began to emerge as well.

The *interest rate* is a significant factor when making investment choices even when, during turbulent times, what is being pursued is currency stability. In fact, exchange rate risk can also be covered on the forward exchange rate market of individual currencies. With respect to the SDR basket, this solution's cost-effectiveness is therefore the most important selection criterion for private operators. It must also be noted that in 1981 the value of the SDR coincided with the dollar's one at about 42 % (just like today), so it was better to use other instruments to hedge dollar risk.

SDR yield was initially set by the IMF with a fixed rate (1.5 % per year, then 5 %). Now, it is set weekly on the basis of the weighted average of the currencies. It forms the basis for the calculation of interest on the Fund's ordinary loans to member countries and interest paid by the Fund on their assets in SDRs and the subscribed quotas.

---

[19] Bank of England, Bank of Belgium and IMF staff estimates. *IMF Paper*, March 1987.

Placing of financial instruments in SDRs in 1981

Instrument	Borrower[20]	Manager	Amount	Maturity	Yield	Date
Syndicated credit	Sweden	Morgan Guaranty	500	5 years	3/8 – ½	I Q
	Ivory Coast	Chase Manhattan	43	8 years	1 ½	I Q
	Ireland	National Westminster	75	10 years	3/8 – ½	II Q
	Cadafe	Chemical	47	6 years	5/8	III Q
	Fenosa	Orion Royal	100	8 years	5/8 – ¾	III Q
	Nafinsa	Chemical	220	8 years	5/8	IV Q
	African Development Bank	Chase Manhattan	200	8 years	½ – 5/8	IV Q
Certificate of deposit	Sumitomo Bank	Chemical	20	3 months	1/8	I Q
	Sanwa Bank	Chemical	20	3 months	1/8	I Q
Floating rate certificate of deposit	Dai-tchi Kangyo Bank	Morgan Stanley	15	2 years	1/8	I Q
	Gulf Bank	Chase Manhattan	15	3 years	¼	I Q
	Fuji Bank	Credit Suisse First Boston	15	3 years	¼	II Q
	Sumitomo Bank	Chemical / Sumitomo Finance	10	3 years	¼	III Q
Eurobond	Nordic Investment Bank	Orion Royal	20	5 years	11.5	I Q
Floating rate commercial paper	ENEL	Dillon Read	100	5 years	¼	I Q
	Pechiney Ugine Kuhlmann	Banque de l'Indochine et de Suez / Kredietbank	50	7 years	¼	II Q
	State Railways	Dillon Read	80	4 years	¼	III Q
	Renfe	Orion Royal	50	8 years	¼	IV Q

---

[20]   Identification in full of the borrowers:
   Cadafe: Compania Anonima de Administration y Fomento Electrico, a Venezuelan state electricity utility

The certificates of deposits were often priced over the three-month LIBOR, while floating rate syndicated credits and commercial paper were usually priced over the six-month LIBOR. The Eurobond yield indicated is equal to the total yield.

In the end, despite the IMF's initial intentions, the basket's main function, until the recent financial crisis, was as a unit of account of the IMF, the BIS and a few other international institutions. The dollar remained the international reserve currency. In 1982, at the outset of globalisation and financial liberalisation, for the first time the US balance of payments recorded a loss in its current accounts (goods and services) as well, whereas before losses were only recorded in the movement of capital. Therefore, this imbalance had to be financed, year after year until today, by attracting capital to the US from the rest of the world, something which severely impacted developing countries.

Using the US dollar as the currency of indebtness is what allowed the US to circumvent budget discipline, requested to any other country by the IMF and the international financial system, and reduce its debt burden through dollar depreciations and cycles of overvaluation and devaluation of liquid and fixed assets denominated in dollars. The US's still undisputed position as the leader of the world economy (we still remember the importance of oil prices in dollars) and their politico-strategic superiority during the Cold War are what made other Western countries accept this asymmetrical relationship.

Building a world system that revolved around an independent currency had to be postponed, but the project to create the European monetary union, already well underway, remained in play and its success has inspired other regional integration efforts, so that it is now possible to propose the original project of SDRs again, with a more level balance of power.

Fenosa: Fuerzas Electrícas del Noroeste, a Spanish private electric utility
Nafinsa: Nacional Financiera, a Mexican state financing agency
ENEL: Ente Nazionale per l'Energia Elettrica, the Italian state electric utility
Pechiney Ugine Kuhlmann, the French multinational
Ferrovie dello Stato, the Italian state railway company
Renfe: Red Nacional de los Ferrocarriles Españoles, the Spanish state railway company.

CHAPTER 4

The Long Life of European Baskets, the EUA and the ECU, up to the Euro (1950-1999)

In the immediate post-war period dollar reserves in European central banks were so depleted that the inconvertibility of their currencies hindered payments, making bartering necessary. Initially, bilateral payment agreements were to be used to tackle this problem; however, they failed to restore trade and distorted trade flows as bilateral credit balances could only be used for purchases in the debtor country.

After being sent to Europe by the IMF in 1947, Triffin set straight to work on a multilateral clearing arrangement: the European Payments Union (EPU).[21] This project was opposed by the US Treasury and the IMF itself, but was greatly appreciated by the State Department. In order to distribute financial aid from the US to Europe (through the "Marshall Plan"), the Organisation for European Economic Cooperation (OEEC) was established, in 1948, with the participation of seventeen countries.[22]

In 1949 the United States suggested that the OEEC create a multilateral agreement; and in 1950 the EPU was set up and replaced bilateral regulations with multilateral clearing. Credit and debit balances, expressed in *European Unit of Account* (EUA) pegged to the dollar, offset each other over time thanks to a credit mechanism funded by the Marshall Plan. The EUA was equal to the gold content of one dollar, like the SDR. Each country received a quota corresponding to 15 % of its total trade with the EPU area and a credit line equal to 60 % of its quota. Credit could be used to a lesser extent as it approached the maximum ceiling. The rest had to be theoretically settled in gold, although in practice this meant in dollars.

---

[21] Ivo Maes and Ilaria Pasotti, "The European Payments Union and the origins of Triffin's regional approach towards international monetary integration", Working Paper Research, National Bank of Belgium, September. 2016, No. 301.

[22] Austria, Belgium, Denmark, France, Great Britain, Greece, Iceland, Ireland, Italy, Luxembourg, Norway, the Netherlands, Portugal, Spain, Sweden, Switzerland and Turkey.

In short, the entire Western monetary system was based on the dollar, which was in turn convertible in gold, as promised by the United States.

The allocation of EPU credits to states was conditional on their adoption of corrective policies. Trade resumption was also fostered by adopting trade liberalisation measures that were also required to join the EPU, mainly consisting in the elimination of all discriminatory measures among participating countries and the progressive lowering of customs barriers. By imposing these conditions on aid, the United States facilitated the first steps towards European integration, but with a monetary system linked to the dollar.

In 1955, given the great success achieved by the EPU, the European Monetary Agreement (EMA) was established, which, in 1958 replaced the EPU. This followed the achievement of full convertibility by some European countries: the six European Economic Community (EEC) countries, Great Britain, the Scandinavian countries, Austria and Portugal. The EMA aimed to continue strengthening monetary and financial cooperation in Europe, and was based on a mechanism for multilateral payment settlement (clearing), which guaranteed the monthly settlement of positive or negative balances at known exchange rates. A European Fund granted discretionary, short-term loans to countries with serious balance of payments difficulties. In December 1972, following an agreement among its member countries, the Organisation for Economic Cooperation and Development (the OECD, no longer the OEEC, which in 1961 ceased to exist) decided to liquidate the European Fund and terminated the EMA by the end of 1972.

Considering the three functions of currency – as a unit of account, a means of payment and a store of value – the EUA fulfilled only the first. Only with a currency unit (the ECU-basket, then the euro as single currency), was Europe able to adopt a monetary policy that was independent of the dollar, as is now the case with the European Central Bank.

In fact, these steps marked the start of a critical phase in European integration, which by 1979, at the crossroads of the customs union crisis and monetary unification, led to the creation of Europe's second basket, the *European Currency Unit* (ECU). Its success was crucial in the decision to convert to a single currency. We discuss this evolution below

In July 1968, just when doubts as to the dollar's convertibility began to emerge, the European Customs Union was completed, a year ahead of the ten-year transitional period provided for in the Rome Treaties, and a decision was made to launch the Common Agricultural Policy: two institutions that would not survive without a fixed exchange rate regime, which the dollar's volatility made impossible to achieve.

At The Hague, in December 1969, the Summit of Heads of State and Government of the European Community (EC) decided to launch the Economic and Monetary Union. This decision resulted in the Werner Plan, which provided for the creation of a European currency after intermediate phases involving the gradual narrowing of fluctuation margins in exchange rates among European currencies. This system, referred to in jargon as the "snake in the tunnel", proved to be insufficient and came under intense strain after the declaration of the dollar's inconvertibility into gold on 15 August 1971. Before the crisis the IMF rules were respected, which allowed for fluctuations in each currency against the dollar by ± 1 % of the declared parity. In reality, many countries, including those of the EC, voluntarily limited this band to ± 0.75 %. In the exchange rate between two European currencies, as a total fluctuation of 1.50 % was possible for each of them against the dollar, there could be a 3 % maximum fluctuation when one of them, e.g. the lira, went from the maximum to the minimum intervention limit and the other, e.g. the D-Mark, went from the minimum to the maximum limit. By extending the permitted fluctuation margins, the paradoxical situation whereby every European currency had a more stable exchange rate against the dollar than other currencies participating in the same economic community was exacerbated. The Werner Plan aimed precisely to reduce maximum oscillation in the cross-rates from 3 % to 1.20 % by July 1971 without affecting the wider oscillation band for the whole EEC monetary bloc against the dollar. However, the aftershock of the crisis in world currency markets, in particular with dollar devaluations and D-Mark revaluations, thwarted this aim.

In June 1970, in Turin, Robert Triffin participated in the conference "For a European Reserve Monetary System", along with Rinaldo Ossola, who had chaired the IMF working group that drew up the proposal to establish the SDR.[23] At the conclusion of the meeting, which brought together two figureheads who had chaired the Union of European Federalists, John Pinder, who had led the British federalists after Lord Beveridge, and Mario Albertini, who was to lead the Italian federalists after Altiero Spinelli, it became clear that SDRs would remain limited as an international liquidity instrument as long as the international system did not evolve into a global balance and

---

[23]   The proceedings of the conference, organised by Centro di Studi e Informazioni (now renamed Centro Einstein di Studi Internazionali) and Istituto Affari Internazionali, were published (in Italian) in the No. 5 of the series *Collana lo Spettatore Internazionale*, with a more explicit title: "Towards a European Currency".

that the priority was therefore to create a European currency. While supporting Robert Triffin's efforts, Mario Albertini in particular understood that creating a single currency would force European governments uphill: towards banking union, a federal budget and a European political power. However, the European single currency was not created to replace the dollar, but rather to create the conditions for a multi-currency monetary system, which could only evolve towards the development of the SDR.

In December 1971 the Washington agreements, in addition to devaluating the dollar for the first time, made it possible to extend fluctuation margins to ± 2.25 % with a 4.50 % maximum variation between each European currency and the dollar. In the above-mentioned example, the lira/mark cross-rate could vary by up to 9 %. On the other hand, applying the narrow fluctuation margin provided for under the Werner Plan, placed into the wider fluctuation band against the dollar, was to trigger paradoxical consequences. For instance, if the lira had fallen to a minimum against the dollar (-2.25 % compared to parity) all the other EC currencies would have had to follow it, thus depreciating. Germany would have had to accept agree to the devaluation of its currency against the dollar despite having a surplus in its balance of payments. Therefore, it was proved that, as expected and foreseen, monetary Europe could not be built simply by narrowing the fluctuation margins among the EC currencies without the closer integration of Member States' economic policies, the management of reserves and controls on capital movements from and to non-EC countries.

In 1975 the EUA (European Unit of Account) was created for the European Development Fund (EDF) and the ECSC (European Coal and Steel Community).

In 1976, as aforementioned, the IMF was reformed by eliminating the fluctuation band and adopting total exchange rate flexibility. In the EC the band was retained to preserve the continuity of the unification project, but it was extended (at times up to 6 %).

However, instead of restoring equality among the various countries and correcting sectoral and regional imbalances, as promised by its supporters, fluctuation of exchange rates magnified pre-existing economic distortions, fuelled inflation, made economies ungovernable and created a hazardous rift among EC countries, undermining the results of the customs union.

The explosion of the contradiction between the common market and fluctuating exchange rates forced governments to take a new step forward towards European unification, but only after making all possible efforts. Consider that there was, by now about ten, both official and private, units of account:

1. Budgetary unit of account
2. Unit of account of the Social Fund
3. Unit of account for the Common Agricultural Policy (CAP)
4. Unit of account for the common customs tariff
5. European Investment Bank's (EIB) unit of account
6. Unit of account for the European Monetary Cooperation Fund (EMCF)
7. Unit of account for the European Development Fund (EDF)
8. Unit of account for the ECSC
9. European Account Unit (EAU)
10. European composite unit of account (EURCO)

We should also add the ECU, which was officially introduced on 13 March 1979, since the replacement of all other units of account by the new currency-basket was not immediate.

The various units of account differed from one another based on the public or private nature of the issuer (e.g., the EURCO was used by the European Investment Bank starting in 1973 to grant loans and issue bonds on the market); for the conversion of units of account/national currencies; for the procedures to change the contents of the basket; to correct the automatic consequences of the unit of account mechanism (e.g. the compensatory allowances for the CAP) and for other special problems posed by the use of each of them.[24]

In the EC the units of account were used:

- to express and measure credits and debits deriving from monetary transactions within the Community;
- to determine the value of financial transactions and maintain the respective value of credits and debits within pre-established periods;
- to establish and maintain a unified price structure in specific sectors, such as agriculture.

The value of the different units of account was determined (not according to the same procedures) following the principle of fixed but adjustable parities. The fixed value, as has been said, corresponded to the gold con-

---

[24]   Giovanni Magnifico, "L'unità di conto europea: considerazioni introduttive", in *Moneta e Credito*, 1976.

tent of the dollar (0.88867088 grammes of fine gold), and the corresponding value in the national currency was adjusted to each change in parity. With the budgetary unit of account linked to the declared monetary parities, which had remained unchanged for many years, the countries whose currency appreciated (or depreciated) contributed more (or less) in their currency to the community budget. At the actual exchange rates Germany would have paid less (in DM) and Italy more (in LIT).

Moreover, the same value of the EUA in gold had become obsolete and abstract after the end of the dollar's convertibility. This explains how and why each of the Communities negotiated specific solutions to their problems (such as compensatory allowances in the case of the CAP). All this sparked constant recriminations and exhausting negotiations that could only be avoided by moving from the unit of account to the basket of currencies. The first of these was the EURCO, which we have already mentioned, introduced in 1973 by the European Investment Bank.

In December 1974 the Commission submitted a proposal to the European Council to replace the units of account with a basket that could: 1) be quoted in the Communities' exchange system and accurately reflect the actual exchange ratios with national currencies; 2) unravel the tangle of different units of account and procedures, thereby achieving a greater degree of transparency not only within the Communities, but also with respect to third countries; 3) create more trust in the unit of account-basket internally and externally; 4) establish a starting point for the strategy to build a European monetary union.[25]

In 1975 the Rome European Council decided to hold the first European elections by direct suffrage in 1979, thus reversing the tendency towards national particularism that had characterised relations among European states in the first half of the 1970s. On 6-7 July 1978, the Bremen European Council launched the European Monetary System (EMS) generating real political change compared to the previous consensus on exchange rate fluctuations, expressed principally by France and Germany.

The association of the direct election of Parliament with the establishment of the EMS had for years been the most immediate demand of federalist, and genuinely progressive economic and social groups throughout Europe, with Italy playing a significant role. In fact, extending the competences of Europe would not have been possible without also increas-

---

25	Commission of the European Communities, "The units of account as a factor of integration", Information Directorate-General – Economy and Finance, No. 87/1975.

ing democratic legitimacy. This was a lesson from the revolution of the American colonists against the British motherland: no taxation without representation.

The EMS introduced a radically different approach to the problem of European monetary stability compared to that of the Werner Plan. It was agreed to adopt the *European Exchange Rate Mechanism* (ERM), establish the *European Monetary Cooperation Fund* (EMCF), transfer resources from rich to poor countries (cohesion policy) and create a parallel currency, the *ECU*, a basket of European currencies which was to be the embryo of the Euro as a single currency.

Currency weights in the ECU (%)

Currency	from 13/03/1979 to 16/09/1984	from 17/09/1984 to 21/09/1989	from 21/09/1989 to 31/12/1998
Danish Crown	3.06	2.69	2.65
Greek Drachma	--	1.31	0.44
Portuguese Escudo	--	--	0.70
Dutch Forint	10.51	10.13	9.98
Belgian Franc	9.64	8.57	8.18
French Franc	19.83	19.06	20.32
Luxembourg Franc	--	--	0.32
Italian Lira	9.49	9.98	7.84
Deutsche Mark	32.98	32.08	31.96
Spanish Peseta	--	--	4.14
Pound Sterling	13.34	14.98	12.45
Irish Pound	1.15	1.20	1.09

The ECU consisted of a fixed amount of each of the twelve national currencies circulating in the Member States at the time of its introduction. Under the Maastricht Treaty, signed in February 1992, this composition was frozen until 1 January 1999. On that date, the ECU was replaced by the *euro*, a single currency and no longer a basket of currencies, at a ratio of 1:1.

The official ECUs were issued by the European Monetary Cooperation Fund through a series of swaps that could be renewed with central banks, which were forced to exchange 20 % of their reserves in gold and dollars for ECUs. In late 1984, due to fluctuations in gold prices and the dollar exchange rate, the ECU supply had more than doubled. Since ECUs were not convertible into the currencies that comprised them, holding ECUs in reserves was equivalent to holding gold or dollars. Three quarters of the ECUs were created against gold.

From 1985 central banks in non-EC countries were allowed to hold ECUs in reserves. To encourage their use, swaps of ECUs/currencies of EC member states were allowed and the ECU's interest rate was raised (from the average of the discount rates to the average rates on the money market of the component currencies).

In 1988 Jacques Delors was re-appointed as Commission President, and proposed structuring the creation of an economic and monetary union in three phases. Following the recommendations of the Report (later known as the Delors Report), the European Council decided that the *first phase* would start on 1 July 1990 with the removal of all restrictions on the movement of capital between Member States. In 1990 the European Council gave greater responsibility to the Committee of Governors of Central Banks (established as early as 1964) to direct the various complex tasks to be carried out by the end of 1993. To implement the second and third phases, it was necessary to amend the Treaty establishing the European Community. The decision was taken by the Intergovernmental Conference on EMU, held in 1991 in conjunction with the Intergovernmental Conference on Political Union, and it was approved in December and signed in Maastricht on 7 February 1992. The Treaty entered into force on 1 November 1993 at the end of the ratification processes of the nation states. It contained, *inter alia*, the Protocol on the Statute of the European System of Central Banks (ESCB) and the European Central Bank (ECB) and the Protocol on the Statute of the European Monetary Institute (EMI).

The creation of the EMI, which took place on 1 January 1994, marked the start of the *second phase* of EMU and led to the dissolution of the Committee of Governors. The EMI, an embryo of the ECB, was tasked with strengthening cooperation between central banks and coordinating monetary policies, and carrying out the necessary preparations to implement a single monetary policy and create a single currency in the third phase. The EMI was not responsible for implementing the monetary policy of the European Union or executing foreign exchange transactions.

The standardisation procedures made two convergences possible: one institutional (national legal orders were adapted, prohibiting *inter alia* the financing of government deficits through central banks) and one economic (aimed at stabilising prices, exchange rates and interest rates in the future euro area). In 1995 the European Council decided to name the single currency the "euro" and confirmed that this process would begin on 1 January 1999. In 1997 it approved the EMI proposals on the principles and fundamental features of the new exchange rate mechanism (ERM II) and adopted the Stability and Growth Pact. On 3 May 1998 it unanimously verified that eleven Member States fulfilled the necessary conditions to adopt the single currency.

Romano Prodi[26] was the President of the Council of Ministers of the Italian Republic and Carlo Azeglio Ciampi,[27] the Secretary of the Treasury. It was agreed that the bilateral central rates of the Member States' currencies would be used to determine the irrevocable conversion rates into euros. Starting on 1 June 1998, when the ECB was established, the EMI concluded its mandate and was dissolved. The preparatory work was completed on schedule and the ECB devoted the remaining months of 1998 to executing the final checks on procedures and systems.

On 1 January 1999 the *third and final phase* of EMU started with the conduct of a single monetary policy, which was the responsibility of the ECB. On 1 January 2002 banknotes also went into circulation. So far eight MS have joined the original eleven, bringing the number of participants to nineteen (twenty-two with the Principality of Monaco, the Republic of San Marino and the Vatican City State).

---

[26] Romano Prodi (1939), an Italian economist, academic and politician, was President of the Council of Ministers twice, from 1996 to 1998 and from 2006 to 2008. He was President of the European Commission from 1999 to 2004. Founder and leader of L'Ulivo, he was President of the National Constituent Assembly of the Democratic Party (2007-2008). On 1 September 2008 he created the Foundation for the Collaboration among Peoples and in October 2012 was appointed Special Envoy of the Secretary General of the United Nations for the Sahel.

[27] Carlo Azeglio Ciampi (1920-2016) began working for the Bank of Italy in 1946 and joined the CGIL (which he left in 1980). He was Governor of the Bank of Italy and President of the Italian Foreign Exchange Office from 1979 to 1993. He was the first non-MP to preside over a technical government (1993-1994). From 1996 to 1999 he was Minister of the Treasury in the governments of Romano Prodi and Massimo D'Alema. The international financial world's trust in him played a decisive role in Italy's entry into the euro. He personally selected the Vitruvian man of Leonardo da Vinci to be portrayed on the Italian one-euro coin, meaning that money is at the service of man and not the opposite. He was the tenth President of the Italian Republic (1999-2006).

CHAPTER 5

The ECU Market (1978-1999): A Model for Relaunching the SDR

Unlike the short-lived SDR market, the ECU market developed into one of the most important sources of support for the single currency. Therefore, it should be examined before looking again at Robert Triffin's argument for a world currency basket, and his theory that in a context completely changed by globalisation and the rebalancing of the different areas of the world, the SDR would be able to play an increasingly important role for cooperative and sustainable governance of the international monetary and financial system.

In 1977 Triffin returned to live in Belgium, left his position at Yale and resumed teaching at his alma mater: the new Université Catholique de Louvain-la-Neuve (UCL). He re-applied for Belgian citizenship while retaining his American citizenship; when he was denied dual citizenship, he opted for Belgium. He worked closely with the European Commission to implement the EMS. Tommaso Padoa-Schioppa[28] was the Director General of the Commission for Economy and Finance from 1979 to 1983. The sentiments of esteem, friendship and trust among people such as Triffin, Padoa-Schioppa and Jacques Delors[29] encouraged their collabo-

---

[28] Tommaso Padoa-Schioppa (1940-2010) worked at the Bank of Italy starting in 1968. After serving on the European Commission (1979-83), he returned to the Bank of Italy as Deputy Director General (1984-1997) and in 1989 participated in the drafting of the Economic and Monetary European Union project on the Delors Committee. He was a member of the Executive Board of the European Central Bank (1998-2006) and Minister of Economy (2006-2008). In the two years that he served as Minister of Economy, Italy's primary surplus climbed from 0.3 % to 3 %, the deficit decreased from 4 % to 2 %, public debt fell from 106.5 % to 104 %, the recovery of unpaid taxes was equal to 20 billion, and investment in infrastructure exceeded 40 billion euros. In October 2007, while he was still Minister under the second Prodi government, he was appointed Chairman of the IMF Ministerial Committee. When he died, he was President of the *Notre Europe* think tank, the association founded by Jacques Delors, later renamed *Institut Jacques Delors* and now chaired by Enrico Letta.

[29] Jacques Delors (1925), after spending his career at the Banque de France and the Commissariat au Plan, was Minister of Economy and Finance under the Mauroy

ration on the launch of the European Monetary System, solving problems that might hinder the establishment of the ECU and designing an economic and monetary union based on the euro.

To explore the possibilities of increasing the role of the SDR in the international monetary system, an interesting starting point is Triffin's thoughts on the European monetary system. He was deeply convinced – as stated in a seminar at the University of Louvain-la-Neuve in 1980 – that the ECU's success depended substantially on the welcome, qualitative and quantitative, that the market would take up the new unit of account, and introduced the formula of the *"open basket"*.

Trading operations in ECU made a quantum leap, as firstly banks and companies, then the States, Belgium and Italy in particular, began to issue bonds.[30] It made a second quantum leap with the development of a day *clearing* system, founded on the initiative of the Belgian Kredietbank and British Lloyds Bank and developed in a multilateral system of ECU banking, based in Paris, in which over forty banks participated, of almost all of EC member states. The Bank for International Settlements of Basel provided the technical structure, following a compromise between central banks that wanted to support the development of the ECU and those that wanted to limit its use. The industrial enterprises created an Association for European Monetary Union.

In 1986, the success of ECU-denominated bonds on the capital markets led the former French President Giscard d'Estaing and the former German Chancellor Helmut Schmidt to resume the initiative to set up the "Committee for the European Monetary Union" including important politicians, industrialists and representatives of the financial sector of the main EC countries. The "Committee", which immediately had a strong impact on the actions of the EC governments, initially seemed to be oriented, in its action, towards supporting the hypothesis of the ECU

Government (President Mitterrand) from 1981 to 1984. From 1985 to 1995 he presided over the European Commission. During his term, the single market was established, the Common Agricultural Policy was reformed and the Single European Act was signed, the latter being the result of Altiero Spinelli's parliamentary commitment to the Constitution, together with the Schengen Agreement and especially the Maastricht Treaty, which established the European Union. In 1994, invited by the Socialist Party to run for president in France, he decided to give up. In 1996 he founded the *Notre Europe* think tank (mentioned in the previous note) which he presided over until 2004. He is still a member of its Board of Directors.

[30]   Public debt issuance in ECUs made it possible for Belgium and Italy to access the international financial market, from which they were *de facto* excluded because of their weak currencies.

as a "parallel currency". However, soon, largely on the basis of the Report written by the former Governor of the Banque de France Renaud de la Genière, the idea prevailed that a "single currency" was needed, issued by a European central bank, instituted by a Treaty. In the following years the programme of the Giscard-Schmidt Committee was implemented step by step, first with the 1988 establishment by the European Council of the Delors Committee and then with the signing of the Maastricht Treaty on February 7, 1992.

Triffin's strategy proved to be a complete success. For sure, today Robert Triffin would devise a new plan to relaunch the SDR under the changed circumstances.[31]

The official features of the ECU soon increased its market appeal. It was considered an "aggressive" financial innovation because it fluctuated less than the weighted sum of the single currencies, reduced transaction costs, was officially recognised in the European Monetary System, could rely on member countries' commitment to defending its stability, was attractive to smaller financial markets as it provided access to products that could only be developed on a larger scale, enabled issuing countries whose currency enjoyed less international confidence to access markets, and acted as a real currency (medium of exchange, unit of account and store of value) despite the absence of a central bank.

Syndicated Loans and Bonds in millions of ECUs

Year	Syndicated Loans	Bond Issues	Number of Issues
1981	230	202	6
1982	367	1,942	19
1983	812	2,547	46
1984	2,780	4,895	66
1985	2,525	12,199	138
1986	1,853	9,381	85
1987	5,091	7,966	72

Source: Istituto Bancario San Paolo di Torino, ECU Newsletter, No. 20[32]

---

[31] Alfonso Iozzo, "From the ECU to the SDR", introduction to the paper by Valentina Tosolini, "The ECU and the SDR: Learning from the Past, Preparing the Future", *RTI-CSF Research Paper*, Turin/Louvain-la-Neuve, November 2014.

[32] V. Tosolini, *op. cit.*, p. 45.

Financial uses of the ECU

Financial instruments	Amounts outstanding (billions)		Growth%
	1991	1989	
* Bonds (national and international):			
- Primary market	124	74	67 %
- Secondary market	(75)	(17)	
* Net assets of banks	176	119	76 %
of which:			
International loans	56	31	81 %
* Euro-paper and treasury bills	18	13	39 %
* Estimate reserves of the central banks	30	17	76 %
* Derived instruments			
MATIF (Paris)	57	Did not exist	
LIFE (London)	13	Did not exist	
FINEX (New York)		23	

Source: Commission of the European Communities, Removing the legal obstacles to the use of the ECU, Brussels 23 December 1992[33]

The fact that markets responded enthusiastically to ECU-denominated issues did not mean that they were initially encouraged by central banks and the banking system. Except for a few innovative bankers, such as Alexandre Lamfalussy[34] (Bank for International Settlements, Basel), Luigi

---

[33]   *Ibid.*, p. 44.

[34]   Alexandre Lamfalussy (1929-2015), a Hungarian-born economist, taught at Yale and Louvain and was Chairman of the Banque de Bruxelles from 1972 until 1975: the year it merged with Banque Lambert becoming Banque Bruxelles Lambert. In 1976 he moved to the Bank for International Settlements, Basel, where he became General Manager (1994-1997) and served as such on the Delors Committee, which was responsible for preparing the single currency. He was the first President of the European Monetary Institute (1994-1997). In 2001 the finance ministers of the Eurozone appointed him as a Chairman of an advisory committee to improve financial market regulation. In 2009 he was charged by his government with restructuring the Belgian financial system, assisted by six experts. In the last years of his life,

Arcuti[35] and Alfonso Iozzo[36] (Istituto Bancario San Paolo di Torino, now Intesa Sanpaolo), few felt that markets would appreciate the ECU issues. The early objections by some bankers, central bankers as well, concerned the complexity of this instrument, the lack of a secondary market, the lack of demand for loans in ECU, the difficulties arising from different national laws and even the supposed competitiveness of the SDR against the ECU. It is interesting to recall, once the same factors in the re-launch of the SDR have been examined in this paper, the short-sighted vision of some banks as opposed to the more forward-looking vision of insurers,

---

he was President of Robert Triffin International and participated actively in all the Foundation's initiatives to reform the international monetary system.

[35] Luigi Arcuti (1924-2013) joined Istituto Bancario San Paolo di Torino in 1945 and later became its General Manager (1974-1980). As President of the IMI (1980), he led the merger with Banca Sanpaolo (1998). He was Chairman of Banca Sanpaolo-IMI (1998-2001) and later appointed Honorary Chairman. Arcuti promoted two paramount initiatives – recalled by Alfonso Iozzo, who was his collaborator and successor – to incorporate the Italian banking system into the European one. In 1979 he proposed that the Bank of Italy and the Ministry of the Treasury spin-off Sanpaolo's banking activities into a limited company, of which the institution responsible for this spin-off, i.e. the "Foundation", would be a shareholder. This would allow the Bank to internationalise by opening up to outside capital and the future company to focus on its historical missions in support of local communities. The idea was welcomed in 1990 under the Amato reform. Convinced that the perverse spiral of inflation and devaluation needed to be stopped, he strongly supported European monetary unification research, granted a loan to the STET in lira but indexed to the ECU and in 1980 accepted Triffin's proposal to facilitate a meeting among European banks to set up the ECU market. The initiative then led to the creation of the ECU Banking Association. Banca Sanpaolo became one of the leading banks in Europe by participating in the launch of the clearing system in cooperation with the BIS. Years later, Arcuti still played a decisive role in the ECU's success by helping to prepare to issue the ECU Treasury bills sought by Minister Andreatta.
Alfonso Iozzo, "Luigi Arcuti, un banchiere per l'Europa", in *Il Sole 24 Ore*, 19 January 2013.

[36] Alfonso Iozzo (1942) joined Istituto Bancario San Paolo di Torino in 1961 and the European Federalist Movement in 1963. At the bank, he was first responsible for the Research and Planning Department and then the Foreign Department. Through the magazine *Thema*, he fostered the formation of a *milieu* of central bankers, economists, financiers and industrialists to reflect on the problems posed by the European integration process. He was the editor of the magazine *ECU Newsletter* (1981-1993), Vice President of the ECU Banking Association (1983-1987) and Chairman of Prometeia (1993-2001). After the merger between Banca Sanpaolo and IMI, he was appointed Managing Director of Banca Sanpaolo-IMI (2001-2006). Finally, he was made President of the Cassa Depositi e Prestiti (2006-2008). Since 2002 he has been Vice President of the Robert Triffin International Foundation (Louvain-la-Neuve).

who because of their profession, are more used to risk assessment over a longer period of time.[37]

At the technical-operational level, the main developments contributing to the development of the market of ECU-denominated financial instruments were:[38]

- The ECU market was linked to the definition of and procedures for the official ECU, which included reviewing its composition every five years so that there was only one ECU used simultaneously in the two circuits and as a unit of account. This was sufficient to dispel any doubts arising from differences in the fixing of exchange rates and interest rates;

- To boost confidence in the basket's stability, the first ECU deposits accepted by Kredietbank were defined based on a closed-basket. The exclusion of variations in the composition of the basket implied, however, the need to limit the duration of contracts. With the expansion of the market, both in the short and long term, open-basket contracts prevailed, and any variations in the composition of the official basket were automatically reflected in the private one;

- in 1983, it was already possible for major banks to quote at any time of the day a spot price against each component currency and against the dollar;

- in the beginning, banks' ECU funding far exceeded ECU loans. This imbalance reached its peak at the end of 1987 (ECU 18.6 billion, 17.7 % of banking assets) and then plummeted (up to 2.3 billion, 1.6 % of assets in September 1990), thanks to the increase in ECU loans and the growing use of the ECU by central banks participating in the EMS, in terms of assets (14 % of total reserves) and foreign exchange market interventions;

- to avoid having to redeem through operating in component currencies, with the attendant increased costs, banks first carried out bilateral clearing, then clearing among a limited group of banks,

---

[37] An example of a very high-level debate on the subject can be found in Atti del Convegno (Proceedings of the Conference) "Un mercato finanziario italiano in euroscudi", Trieste, 21 March 1981, in *Quaderni dell'Istituto per gli Sudi Assicurativi*, No. 34. In particular, regarding the insurers' position, which may be equated with that of pension fund managers, see Alfonso Desiata's report "L'euroscudo nei rapporti assicurativi", in *Bancaria*, 1981

[38] For a complete description of what is summarised here, see V. Tosolini, *op. cit.*

one of which subsequently carried out the *nettoyage*, with the ECU
Banking Association and the Bank for International Settlements
organising the final ECU clearing system, which was multilateral,
world-wide, open, fully computerised and equipped with a supranational clearing centre (neutral with respect to individual banks).
In this way, the creation/redemption of the ECU *vis-à-vis* individual currencies was limited to net balances; national central banks
had no trouble playing the last-resort lender (in case of market
liquidity shortages).

During the 1980s political problems were also gradually solved. Here,
we shall only report the preliminary issue and the final stage.

The former arose regarding the status that should be granted to the
ECU. In 1981 the Italian Ministry of Foreign Trade had already recognised
the ECU as a "currency". Moreover, the Bank of Italy not only recognised
it as a foreign currency, but treated it as such, by including it in its reserves.
Soon a third of Italian public debt was denominated in ECUs. However, in
Germany the longstanding opinion was that the ECU was the equivalent
of an indexation clause and was prohibited in financial contracts due to
the indelible mark left by the Weimar Republic's hyper-inflation followed
by deflation, Nazism and war. However, German banks' entry into the
market was then to contribute greatly to its development and influence
authorities' thinking.[39]

The latter concerned removing the remaining obstacles to market
development and launching the basket as a real currency, when in 1989
the Madrid European Council decided to implement the first phase of
the Delors Report starting on 1 January 1990: "the Community will
have a single currency – a strong and stable ECU – which will be an
expression of its identity and unity". Despite remaining ambiguities
between the single currency and basket – because at the time there
were still doubts as to whether or not the pound, which was part of the
ECU, would be part of this plan – the measures actually taken removed
the final obstacles to the private use of the ECU, making it impossible

---

[39]   In this regard, we cannot forget the crucial role played by German banker Alfred
Herrhausen (1930-1989), then Head of the Deutsche Bank. An extraordinarily com-
petent person with a unique sense of history. Herrhausen is known for proposing
that the International Monetary Fund and the World Bank reduce Third World debt
and for his vision of the role his Bank would have to play to foster the development
of East and West Germany after reunification, which had to be balanced and open
to relations with Moscow. Less well known is his essential contribution to securing
Germany's support.

to change its composition. At that time, the ECU market, which had been growing continuously since 1987, was worth ECU 300 billion. After this step, long-term (over ten year) bond issues in ECU increased sharply, while they had never been significant or in 1988 and 1989 had even reduced to zero. In the years 1990-1991, total bond issues of any maturity increased by 49 %.[40]

Long-term bond issues

Year of Issue	ECUs (expressed in millions)
1982	60
1983	220
1984	535
1985	623
1986	760
1987	175
1988	0
1989	0
1990	2,950
1991	3,946
1992	3,650
Total	12,919

Source: ECU Newsletter

The Maastricht Treaty (1992) marked the final transition from the ECU-basket to the ECU-currency. Not all the members proceeded at the same pace of economic and fiscal convergence and with the same criteria throughout the 1980s, but those who are still worried about the possibility of a multi-speed Europe should be heartened by the fact that all the EMS countries were ready for the single currency on 1 January 1999 (except for Britain and Denmark, which signed the Maastricht Treaty with an opting out clause, and Greece, which joined the euro in 2001).

Today, the euro is the second largest currency in the world, accounting for 22 % of international loans, 29 % of global payments and 20 % of official

---

[40]   V. Tosolini, *op. cit.*, pp. 65-68.

foreign reserves. 340 million Europeans in nineteen Member States share it. Sixty countries and territories, representing another 175 million people, have pegged their currencies to the euro. Public support for the single currency is at its highest (72 % of favourable opinions)[41] since its creation.

---

[41] ECB data June 2016, the European Commission and Eurobarometer 2017, taken from European Commission, "Reflection Paper on the Deepening of the Economic and Monetary Union", Brussels, 31 May 2017.

CHAPTER 6

IMF Reform after the Crisis: The Increase in Quotas and the SDR Allocation (2009-2016)

In the first half of the decade that opened the 21st century animal spirits were raging on Wall Street under the sign of bull. Capital flowed into the United States from all over the world to capture an upturn in the market, and then another as markets continued to soar. The crisis that was to then force everybody to read up on finance – for professional development or just to find out why they had lost their savings – seemed remote, or even impossible.

Yet some think tanks, without worrying about which form the crisis might take, sensed this in the fundamentals of the American economy: the current balance of payments deficit which had been persistent, cumulative and uninterrupted since 1982, budget deficit and public debt, and unsustainable growth in net foreign debt.

The financial crisis affected the United States in 2007 after bleeding the peripheral countries for a long time: from Japan to South-East Asia, from Russia to investors in the LTCM Fund, from Mexico to Argentina, from the failure of WorldCom to the Enron scandal.

The crisis that hit the United States came as a result of now-notorious uncollectible *sub-prime* loans, i.e. a loose way of granting credit to families, which had the effect of doubling the real (deflated) price of buildings used as collateral for the mortgages themselves.[42] The illusion of wealth made it possible to grant mortgages even to those who normally would not have been considered creditworthy according to ordinary assessment

---

[42] Robert J. Fischer's indices, published regularly in the American financial press, would have been sufficient to sound the alarm even earlier than the usual rise in interest rates and the end of the ultra-permissive monetary policy followed by Alan Greenspan. Moreover, a look at the US balance of payments and public debt could give rise to some questions about how the United States systematically funded the realisation of the American dream with wars, despite wage stagnation and tax reduction for the highest income brackets. Queen Elizabeth should not have been asking why economists did not foresee the crisis, but why the minority who did foresee it was not listened to.

standards. These loans were secured through the shadow banking system (through bank derivatives created to escape the few residual checks after deregulation) which had various ways of packaging and mixing the more or less collectible loans so they could offer customers a varied range of products with a risk/return range to suit any preference. These composite securities, whose content was sometimes indecipherable for the issuers themselves, were also offered to European banks, which unfortunately agreed to accumulate them, thus bringing the crisis to Europe.

The effects of the financial crisis quickly spread to the real economy through a number of channels. In Europe, the main effects were:

- economic activity, international trade and employment decreased;
- families became poorer and inequality increased;
- credit to businesses was restricted (the credit crunch) to reduce leverage between banks' own funds and loans granted (deleveraging);
- consumer propensity, risk and investment decreased as a result;
- public finances worsened due to lower revenues, economic recession and major expenditures, automatic buffers and Keynesian policies to support the economy and rescue the most vulnerable banks.

Regarding the crisis, which has been examined carefully in the extensive literature, it is interesting to remember how it triggered a resurgence of interest in a stable, independent, cooperative and sustainable currency and how difficult it was for President Obama to obtain Congress' approval to reform the IMF and support the modification of the SDR basket by including the Chinese currency.

On 15 September 2008 in New York the Lehman Brothers Holdings announced its intention to file for bankruptcy protection referred to in Chapter 11. It was the largest banking failure in history. The leaders of the Group of Twenty met in London on 2 April 2009.

The summit's final *communiqué* contained agreed guidelines for a recovery from the crisis. First of all, the summit concluded that "a global crisis requires a global solution" and "prosperity is indivisible." For "sustainable globalisation" and rising prosperity to be achieved, the market economy needed to be combined with strong global institutions and effective regulation. Therefore, the leaders committed themselves to taking all necessary actions together to restore confidence, growth and jobs, support the financial system, strengthen the rules (re-regulation), reform and recapitalise financial institutions, promote global trade and investment by rejecting protectionism and stimulating an inclusive, green and sustainable recovery.

Regarding the international monetary and financial system, at the London summit a total intervention of 1,100 billion was agreed (all the figures in the G20 *communiqué* are expressed in dollars) in order to:

- triple the IMF's available resources (quotas) from 250 to 750 billion (+500, of which 250 paid immediately and another 250 with a subsequent extension of the Agreements to Borrow);
- support a new SDR allocation (+250 billion);
- support additional lending by the Multinational Development Banks – MDBs (+100 billion);
- grant new trade financing (+250 billion);
- in addition, use additional resources from gold sales, already agreed, for concessional financing of the poorest countries.

These interventions, together with expansionary budgetary policies at the level of individual states equal to $5,000 billion in the two-year period from 2009 to 2010, constituted "concerted and unprecedented fiscal expansion," accompanied by accommodative monetary policies.

Regarding national expansion policies, these were possible only in the United States, which could easily finance the debt created because of the hegemony of the dollar.

The decisions on the increase in the IMF's quotas and the new allocations in SDRs are different in their meaning and process. Along with the inclusion of the renminbi in the SDR basket, covered in the next chapter, they suffered the common fate of being blocked by the US Congress until autumn 2015, and then approved in 2016. Barack Obama, who had already expressed his consent at the 2009 G20, had to wait until the end of the two presidential terms to obtain their approval.

In addition to acknowledging Obama's legacy – without whom no progress could be made today – honourable mention should be given to the preparatory work carried out by the IMF headed by Dominique Strauss-Kahn[43] (2007-2011).

---

[43]　Dominique Strauss-Kahn (1949) was minister several times in economic departments in Socialist-led governments. Under the François Mitterrand Presidency he was Minister of Industry and Foreign Trade (1991-1993) in the Édith Cresson and Pierre Bérégovoy governments and Minister of Economy, Finance and Industry in the Lionel Jospin government (1997-1999). After Jacques Chirac's victory in 2002

The member countries' quotas, based on their relative weight in the world economy,[44] perform many functions:

- They constitute the country's maximum financial commitment to the Fund, which must be paid upon subscription: up to 25 % in SDRs or in widely accepted currencies, such as the five components of the basket, and 75 % in national currency;
- They largely determine members' voting power, which includes basic votes plus an additional vote for each SDR100,000 of quota;[45]
- They are the reference for determining the country's access limit to the Fund's financing.[46]

Any changes in quotas must be approved by an 85 % majority of the total voting power. A country's quota cannot be changed without its consent. A general quota review theoretically takes place every five years, assessing the total quotas necessary to finance member countries' balances

---

(Jospin did not even qualify for the second round being surpassed by Le Pen), he set up the Reflection Group with Michel Rocard *A gauche en Europe* and chaired the reform-oriented Socialist Party faction *Socialisme et Démocratie*. In July 2007 he was officially nominated as a candidate for the IMF Directorate General by Nicolas Sarkozy, and was appointed and took office on 1 November. Over the years of its commitment to the Fund, he has introduced radical changes in its ideological orientations, replacing a Keynesian approach to the then dominant liberal one (the Washington Consensus). Studies carried out at his request in view of the relaunch of the SDR were valuable in the years of crisis and the subsequent need for international liquidity, and still today illuminate the road ahead. In April 2011, a speech given at the Brookings Institution in which he openly proposed to combat future inequality through a return to full employment and public investment, created a stir within the IMF. He was arrested on 14 May 2011 in New York for a sex scandal and resigned from the Fund four days later. On 23 August the New York district attorney dismissed all charges against him.

[44]   The current formula to determine relative weight in the world economy is the weighted average of GDP (which weights of 50 %, in turn measured for 60 % based on market exchange rates and 40 % on PPA exchange rates), international openness (30 %), economic variability (15 %) and international reserves (5 %). The formula also includes a "compression factor" to reduce the dispersion in calculated quota shares.

[45]   The 2008 reforms tripled the number of basic votes to 5.502 % of the total votes, thus strengthening the voice of poor countries. They strengthened the participation of emerging economies through ad hoc quota increases for 54 member countries. These came into force on 3 March 2011.

[46]   For instance, under Stand-By and Extended Arrangements, a member can borrow up to 145 % of its quota annually and up to 435 % cumulatively. Access to credit may also be higher in certain circumstances.

of payments and the distribution in the increase among the members in relation to the changes in their relative positions.

In December 2010, the Board of Governors, the IMF's highest decision-making body, completed the *14th General Review of Quotas* (and voting rights) which:

- doubled quotas from SDR 238.5 billion to SDR 477 billion (this was the first $250 million increase agreed at the G20);
- transferred over 6 % of the voting rights from over-represented Members to under-represented ones;
- significantly realigned quotas, making China the third most important country in the Fund and placing another three emerging countries among the top ten (Brazil, India and Russia);
- preserved the quotas and voting rights of the poorest countries.[47]

For the reasons already explained, the reform package did not come into force until 2016, and subsequently the United States, with 17.46 % of the quotas and 16.53 % of voting rights, retained its veto power on all decisions requiring an 85 % majority. Regarding the other four component currencies of the SDR basket, the Eurozone countries hold, overall, 22.3 % of quotas and 21.68 % of voting rights, China 6.41 % and 6.09 % respectively, Japan 6.48 and 6.16 and the United Kingdom 4.24 and 4.04. Therefore, the countries also represented in the SDR basket hold 56.89 % of the quotas and 54.5 % of voting rights. The three emerging countries that have yet to be represented in the basket are India, with 2.76 % of quotas and 2.64 % of voting rights, the Russian Federation, with 2.71 % and 2.59 %, and Brazil with 2.32 % and 2.22 %. Only two other countries exceed 2 % participation: Canada and Saudi Arabia. Until the Eurozone reaches its goal of unitary representation in the Fund as set out in the programme of the Juncker Commission, it will have no veto rights and, most importantly, the only way for it to implement effective initiatives will be by making strenuous agreements with nineteen countries.

In December 2016, the Board of Governors invited the Executive Committee to proceed promptly in the preparation of the *15th General Revision of Quotas* with the aim of ending the work by 2019.

---

[47]   These countries were defined as those which were eligible for the Poverty Reduction and Growth Trust (PRGT) and with a per capita income below $1,135 in 2008 (or twice that amount for smaller countries).

Let us consider the allocation of SDRs. *General* allocations must be justified by a global long-term need to increase reserve instruments. Decisions are made for 5-year periods (the last report is dated June 2016). So far there have been only three: the first for SDR 9.3 billion (1970-72), the second for 12.1 billion (1979-81) and the third for 161.2 billion (28 August 2009). Separately, the Fourth Amendment to the Articles of the Agreement, which became effective on 10 August 2009, provided for a *special* 21.5-billion allocation to allow all members to participate in SDR allocations and compensate for the fact that the countries that joined the IMF after 1981 (more than one fifth of the current IMF members) did not receive any SDR allocations until 2009. The cumulative allocation thus reached a total of SDR 204.1 billion.

CHAPTER 7

China's Return to the World Economy Culminating in the Inclusion of the Renminbi in the SDR basket (2016)

Considering China's rise to the top of the world economy in recent decades as an extraordinary and unpredictable phenomenon – a kind of tsunami – would be completely wrong. Rather, this should be seen as China's *return* to its place in the world, with the weight it has had for millennia, and as the end of the historical *stasis* gripping China for two centuries. There is a great deal of literature that focuses on the underlying reasons for this, and China's return.

Today *economic statistics* make it possible to compare economic variables even over a thousand-year timespan, in particular based on the method of purchasing power parity (PPP). Maddison's data, which only reports on a few relevant years in the last two centuries, show that China's contribution to world GDP (PPP) and population in 1820, i.e. before the effects of the industrial revolution were felt, was substantially balanced, with a 32.9 % share of world GDP and 36.6 % of the population.

In 1913, on the eve of the First World War, China's share in world GDP had fallen to 8.8 %, and population was 24.4 %. In 1950, the first year of peace after the Second World War, its world GDP share was reduced to 4.5 % while its population remained relatively stable at 21.7 %. It took half a century to improve the situation when in 2001 GDP rose to 12.3 % and population went down to 20.7 %.

The most recent data have been taken from the *World Economic Outlook Database* of the IMF, according to which China's contribution to world GDP (always based on PPA, thus comparable to Maddison's long series) was estimated at 17.8 % in 2016 and at 18.3 % in the forecasts for 2017, while its population dropped to 18.5 %. A sort of equilibrium has actually been regained, and its share of world income is close to its share of population, but the inequality gap between urban and rural areas has widened between the first and last income deciles.

World GDP shares (PPA %)

	1820	1913	1950	2001
Europe (excluding the UK)	21.4	29.2	17.2	19.1
UK	5.2	8.2	6.5	3.2
Former USSR	5.4	8.5	9.6	3.6
United States	1.8	18.9	27.3	21.4
Other Western countries	0.1	2.4	3.4	3.2
Latin America and Mexico	2.2	4.4	7.8	8.3
Asia (excluding Japan and China)	23.5	13.5	10.9	18.6
Japan	3.0	2.6	3.0	7.1
China	32.9	8.8	4.5	12.3
Africa	4.5	2.9	3.8	3.3
WORLD	100.0	100.0	100.0	100.0

World population shares (%)

	1820	1913	1950	2001
Europe (excluding the UK)	14.3	16.5	13.6	7.4
UK	2.0	2.5	2.0	1.0
Former USSR	5.3	8.7	7.1	4.7
United States	1.0	5.4	6.0	4.6
Other Western countries	0.1	0.8	1.0	0.9
Latin America and Mexico	2.1	4.5	6.6	8.6
Asia (excluding Japan and China)	28.6	27.3	29.7	36.7
Japan	3.0	2.9	3.3	2.1
China	36.6	24.4	21.7	20.7
Africa	7.1	7.0	9.0	13.4
WORLD	100.0	100.0	100.0	100.0

Source: Angus Maddison, *The World Economy*, OECD, 2006.

Finally, China's contribution to world GDP in current monetary terms is equal to 15.1 % for 2016 – which is less useful for comparison but essential to calculate financial ratios, such as the debt/GDP ratio. According to the Fund's forecasts, in 2017 China was expected to contribute to growth (i.e. to the world's highest nominal GDP compared to that of 2016) by

22 %, confirming its role as the primary driver of world development, despite the current slowdown.

Thanks to its development over the last thirty years, China can assume increasing responsibility in international institutions, and particularly in the IMF, where it is currently the third country, with 6.41 % of quotas. The need to proceed, albeit gradually, towards a greater autonomy of local entities is becoming more pressing and more probable.

The Chinese presidency of the G20 in 2016 and China's One Belt One Road (OBOR) initiative have provided global reach to the grand and responsible design for openness towards, and connection with, the other regions of Asia, Europe and Africa, which is part of a colossal investment programme. In particular, Africa represents a common Euro-Chinese interest in many respects, including local development and migration control, agriculture and the food industry, energy and finance for the "real" economy.

The international importance of the *renminbi* is not yet proportional to China's economic power. China produces 15 % of world GDP, accounts for 13 % of international trade and holds 30 % of official global reserves. On the other hand, the renminbi accounts for less than 3 % of global international payments for commercial and financial transactions and for less than 2 % of total exchange market transactions,[48] Its modest circulation is due to its lack of a developed banking system and the controlled exchange regime.

The Chinese currency was pegged to the dollar until 2005, when it announced its will to anchor its exchange rate, not to a single currency, but to a basket representative of the actual exchanges with various countries. This change caused the renminbi to appreciate considerably. China has thus been the first surplus country in history to make "symmetrical rebalancing" possible, as desired by Keynes and Triffin. Between 2007 and 2015, the effective renminbi exchange rate (i.e. against the various currencies with their relative weight in Chinese trade) and the real exchange rate (i.e. net of inflation differentials) appreciated by around 45 %. However, China is still criticised for controlling capital movements. But the Chinese government cannot shift away from the current managed floating regime of the renminbi to a free floating regime because Chinese savers' demand

---

[48] 2015 data of the international payment system SWIFT. Only with the IMF's subsequent publication of data on reserves will the weight of the renminbi in the reserves of other countries be known for the first time.

for portfolio diversification would fuel capital flows from China to foreign countries. Prometeia points out that in 2016 and in the first half of 2017:

> The slowdown in growth and the strength of the dollar are putting pressure on capital outflows and the depreciation of the [Chinese] currency that untimely liberalisation might render uncontrollable... From 2014 onwards, several steps have been taken towards the internationalisation of the yuan, both through the increased number of non-Chinese players admitted to onshore trading and the permitted share of investments, and through the establishment of bilateral markets and facilities in some financial centres for direct exchanges of the yuan, for example with the euro and the pound sterling... The monetary authority is slowed down by the fact that over the last year and a half the yuan has suffered a depreciation of 11.3 % against the dollar... despite interventions of about 1000 billion dollars of reserves, about a quarter of the total... The depreciation of the yuan against the dollar [stands] against the almost total stability of the reference baskets [SDR, actual exchange rate calculated by the BIS and basket calculated by the PBoC].[49]

The basket calculated by the People's Bank of China (PBoC), to fix the renminbi (RMB) exchange rate, has witnessed the continued erosion of the dollar's weight. After the last change, at the end of 2016, this fell to 22.40 % (while it still weighs 41.73 % in the SDR basket, despite the inclusion of the RMB with a weight of 10.92 %). The weights of the other major currencies in the PBoC basket are: euro 16.34 % (30.93 in SDRs), yen 11.53 % (8.33 in SDRs), Korean won 10.77 % (not included in SDRs). The remaining 38.96 % is divided among 20 other currencies, each of which weighted less than 5 %. Among these, the pound sterling weighs 3.16 % (8.09 in the SDR).

The multiplication of international baskets reminds us of the large number of EUA created in Europe for different purposes, before the advent of the ECU. The current risk is that the international monetary system that is now being defined is not only multi-currency, but also multi-basket. This is one more reason to strengthen the use of the SDR. The first step towards creating a world currency is the creation of a single basket, similar to the ECU in the preparatory phase for the creation of the euro. In March 2009, in the height of the crisis, the Governor of the PBoC Zhou Xiaochuang proposed using an existing tool, the SDR, by changing its composition, making it possible to convert it into other currencies, promoting its use in international trade, in the quotation of raw materials and in the accounts of transnational companies, allowing

---

49   Prometeia, *Forecast Report*, Bologna, March 2017, pp. 46-47 (Own translation).

SDR-denominated bonds to be issued, equipping the IMF with a pool of reserves to strengthen market confidence in its value.

The acceptance of credit-based national currencies as major international reserve currencies, as is the case in the current system, is a rare special case in history. [...] The Triffin Dilemma, i.e., the issuing countries of reserve currencies cannot maintain the value of the reserve currencies while providing liquidity to the world, still exists. [...] The price is becoming increasingly higher, not only for the users, but also for the issuers of the reserve currencies. Although crisis may not necessarily be an intended result of the issuing authorities, it is an inevitable outcome of the institutional flaws. The desirable goal of reforming the international monetary system, therefore, is to create an international reserve currency that is disconnected from individual nations and is able to remain stable in the long run, thus removing the inherent deficiencies caused by using credit-based national currencies. [...] Keynes had already proposed to introduce an international currency unit named "Bancor", based on the value of 30 representative commodities. Unfortunately, the proposal was not accepted. The collapse of the Bretton Woods system, which was based on the White approach, indicates that the Keynesian approach may have been more farsighted. The IMF also created the SDR in 1969, when the defects of the Bretton Woods system initially emerged, to mitigate the inherent risks sovereign reserve currencies caused. Yet, the role of the SDR has not been put into full play due to limitations on its allocation and the scope of its uses. However, it serves as the light in the tunnel for the reform of the international monetary system. [...] A super-sovereign reserve currency managed by a global institution could be used to both create and control the global liquidity. [...] This will significantly reduce the risks of a future crisis and enhance crisis management capability. [...] The reform should be guided by a grand vision and begin with specific deliverables. It should be a gradual process that yields win-win results for all. [...] In the short run, the international community, particularly the IMF, should at least recognize and face up to the risks resulting from the existing system, conduct regular monitoring and assessment and issue timely early warnings. Special consideration should be given to giving the SDR a greater role. The SDR has the features and potential to act as a super-sovereign reserve currency. [...] This will require political cooperation among member countries. [...] The scope of using the SDR should be broadened, so as to enable it to fully satisfy the member countries' demand for a reserve currency. [...] Compared with separate management of reserves by individual countries, the centralized management of part of the global reserve by a trustworthy international institution with a reasonable return to encourage participation will be more effective in deterring speculation and stabilizing financial markets. The participating countries can also save some reserve for domestic development and economic growth. With its universal membership, its unique mandate of maintaining monetary and financial stability, and as an international "supervisor" on the macroeconomic policies of its member countries, the IMF, equipped with its expertise, is endowed with a natural advantage to act as the manager of its member countries' reserves. The centralized management of its member countries' reserves by the Fund will be an effective measure to promote a greater role of the SDR as a reserve currency. To achieve this, the IMF can set up an open-ended SDR-denominated fund based on the market practice, allowing subscription and redemption in the existing reserve currencies by various investors as desired. This arrangement will not only promote the development of SDR-denominated assets, but will also partially allow management of the liquidity in the form of the existing reserve currencies. It can even lay a foundation for increasing SDR allocation to gradually replace existing reserve currencies with the SDR.[50]

The cooperation called for by Zhou is essential to managing globalisation and preventing it, if left to market forces alone, from threatening democracy, free trade and peace. The consolidation of China's position in the IMF has a valuable reforming potential, but as it seems unlikely that any additional official reforms of the international monetary system[51] will be agreed with the United States, and as was the case for the ECU, this makes the preliminary distribution of the SDR in financial markets necessary.

The renminbi's contribution to the new system requires the gradual expansion and strengthening of financial markets. The Chinese monetary authorities – like the German ones when the mark was playing an international role – suggest preventing the formation of a destabilising offshore renminbi market (Hong Kong)[52] and fostering the slower but more robust and controllable development of an *onshore* market (Shanghai).

---

[50]　Zhou Xiaochuang, "Reform the international monetary system", *BIS Review*, 41/2009.

[51]　An example of the new climate, and the old objections, can be found in the article by Benjamin J. Cohen, "Should China Be Ejected from the SDR?", *Project Syndicate*, 30 May 2017.

[52]　On 1 July 1997, the UK transferred sovereignty over Hong Kong to China, with a transitional period of 50 years during which a model was to be applied by Deng Xiaoping referred to as "one country, two systems", to indicate China's respect for the "democratic" rules of the British regime, including its very permissive financial scheme. In the early years, this allowed Hong Kong to act as an offshore centre. However, the increasing internationalisation of the renminbi has also forced the Hong Kong Stock Exchange to sign agreements with China to avoid being excluded from the Shanghai onshore market, accepting the rules. Many expect a fusion of the two markets even before the expiry of the transitional period. The offshore strategy, similar to what Theresa May would like to implement for the City with respect to the "Continent", has not turned out to be true.

As to the increase in trade with China, many Asian countries peg their currencies to the renminbi, thus facilitating its establishment also as a reserve currency in the area.[53]

In 2016, when the inclusion of the renminbi in the SDR basket became operational, the World Bank announced an agreement with the People's Bank of China for a two billion SDR issue (equal to USD 2.8 billion) on the Chinese domestic market, payable in renminbi. The first tranche of SDR 500 million (approximately USD 700 million) was launched in early September 2016 (with a three-year maturity and an annual coupon of 0.49 %). The issue reminds us of those made in ECU on domestic markets first by Italy and then Belgium and France. Subsequently, the private bank Standard and Chartered Bank also placed an issue for SDR 100 million. The SDR issue of the World Bank offers a means of diversification that is different from the dollar, as it is more secure and more stable, for Chinese savings.

The example could be followed by regional development banks and private issuers. At the 2017 IMF and World Bank Spring Meetings, Vice-Governor Yi Gang declared that the PBoC was starting to draw up balance of payments and reserve reports in SDR and hoped that other market institutions would do the same to encourage participation in the market to increase its liquidity. Yi also highlighted the role played by the IMF in the new SDR allocations and underlined how the same role could be played by the issuing countries of the current reserve currencies to facilitate the SDR/other currencies exchange. In the same meetings, Allianz's chief economic advisor Mohamed El-Erian also suggested that multilateral banks, sovereign wealth funds and multinational companies operate on the SDR market.

On 13 June 2017 the ECB announced that it had invested EUR 500 million in renminbi, leaving total reserves unchanged and reducing the share of reserves held in dollars (which still remain the largest) by the same value. Among the reasons, the ECB press release cites: the increased use of the renminbi in international reserves, the recognition by the IMF that the renminbi is a freely usable currency, its inclusion in the SDR basket, the importance of China as one of the major commercial partners of the European Union.

As of 26 June 2017 Chinese quoted companies shares contribute to the formation of the global stock exchange index.

---

[53] Miriam Campanella, "The Internazionalization of the Renminbi and the Rise of a Multipolar Currency System", *ECIPE Working Paper*, No. 01/2014.

CHAPTER 8

The Multi-Currency System
and the Future of the SDR

The frightful storm that started in 2007 is not completely over, and the signs of a forthcoming crisis are already making economists anxious This time, any significant destabilisation in the integrated international financial market will not be remedied by another extension of central banks' assets, after the unprecedented one already implemented by the Fed, the ECB, the BoE and the BoJ, which today would require a more gradual tapering. Yet Anglo-Saxon countries' current account deficit – which continues to rise unchecked – does not give us any hope that a new balance will be achieved in the current international monetary system.[54]

Current Account 2016 (% of Global GDP)

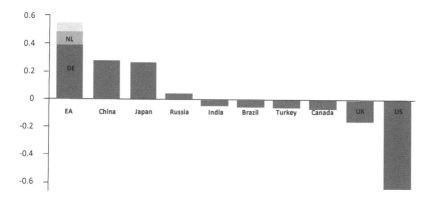

Security cannot be sought by returning to the beginning, i.e. to the (inconvertible) dollar-standard, nor can it be replaced by a renminbi or

---

[54] The graph (EU Commission's calculations based on IMF data) is taken from Marco Buti's "Triffin Lecture" in Brussels, on 6 June 2017 – see also Marco Buti "The New Global Economic Governance. Can Europe Help Win the Peace?", *RTI-CSF Research Paper* (prepared as follow up of the above cited Triffin Lecture), Turin/Louvain-la-Neuve, July 2017.

euro-standard, because today there is a balanced distribution of economic weight across different areas in the world. The dollar, the renminbi, the euro, and other currencies to a lesser extent will play a regional, not global, role to avoid falling prey to the "Triffin dilemma", as Zhou pointed out in his 2009 article. Therefore, it is necessary to follow the path already blazed by Keynes and Triffin. Since then many things have changed, but not the *direction* of necessary change. In *Alice in Wonderland*, when Alice asks how to get out, the cat replies: "It depends where you want to go." Thanks to our predecessors, we know where we want to go. Yes, the world has become more complex, as happens in regime transitions, and the sea is stormier. However, our ships are faster, our tools more powerful and communication with skippers faster.

The current international monetary system is multi-currency, with three main currencies (the dollar, the euro and the renminbi) and two that are less common (the yen and the pound). Many of the other currencies are variously linked to the first five. In addition, several baskets are used by some countries, including China.

The system is structured like this because of two reasons and one restriction. The first reason, as we have seen, is the de-dollarisation process, initiated by creating the ECU, then the euro – pursued as a sort of return to the gold standard in terms of the inspiration underpinning the policies of some oil-exporting countries – and by incorporating local currencies and ad hoc baskets into foreign exchange and Asian reserve policy. The second, is a result of globalisation, which has sped up the rebalancing of the weights of the various regions in the world economy and has increased intra-regional, even more than inter-regional, trade.

Replacing the dollar as the international currency with other national or supranational currencies can help stabilise currency and finance regional areas of high-level economic integration and must therefore be encouraged, but it does not meet the requirements of a world currency.[55] To explore this problem the IMF defined the three roles of the SDR,[56] which clearly represent the three functions of currency: unit of account; official

---

[55]   The problems related to the multi-currency system and the need to peg currencies, at the national and international level, have been highlighted by the BIS head of the Monetary and Economic Department: Claudio Borio, "More Pluralism, More Stability?", presentation at the Seventh High-level SNB-IMF Conference on the International Monetary System, May 2016.

[56]   IMF, "The Role of the SDR – Initial Considerations", Staff Notes for the G20, Washington, 15 July 2016.

reserve instrument (O-SDR); and public or private financial instruments placed on the market (M-SDRs).

The SDR is used as a *unit of account* for economic statistics, financial statements and transaction pricing. China and International Financial Statistics publish international reserve data in SDR. A number of international institutions, including the BIS, and regional institutions use the SDR as a unit of account for their balance sheets and some multilateral banks denominate their loans in SDR. The SDR is also used to price some multinational transactions, such as transit permits in the Suez Canal (since 1975), compensation for lost baggage by airlines under the Montreal Convention and the International Postal Union tariffs. Overall, as the Fund notes, the use of the SDR as a unit of account has not developed as it might have, as it would be useful to reduce variations in value due to exchange rate fluctuations.

In fact, the US did not even facilitate the use of the SDR as cash, fearing this would weaken the dollar's status as the only international reserve currency. An example was when the OPEC countries announced (Libreville, Gabon, 11 June 1975) the decision to adopt the SDR as a unit of account, which, however, was not then followed up, thanks to Saudi Arabia's agreement to continue fixing the price of oil in dollars.

The price of raw materials is less volatile when priced in SDRs than in dollars. The uncertainties resulting from the five-year review of the SDR basket are overestimated because, conversely, this periodic adjustment contributes to its long-term stability.[57] A simulation carried out by Robert Triffin International (RTI)[58] shows a negative correlation between the dollar exchange rate and the price of two essential raw materials: crude oil and wheat; while the quotation given in a supranational currency such as the SDR would reduce speculation and price variability.

In the short term, when the dollar depreciates, *commodities* attract investors who are paying off future inflation and protecting themselves from the weakening of the dollar. This results in the greater financialisation of goods, starting with oil. In the long term, results depend on market power. Exporters will attempt to increase prices to compensate for the devaluation of the dollar while supply and demand will become more flexible because there will be enough time to plan investments to increase

[57] *Ibid.*, pp. 12-13.
[58] Valentina Tosolini, "Analysing Commodity Prices: Trend for Crude Oil and Wheat in US Dollars, Euro and SDR", *op. cit.*

production capacity and/or look for surrogates for the goods under pressure, thereby reducing their consumption.

In conclusion, it may be said that, on average and *ceteris paribus*, the dollar's devaluation tends to reduce the price of oil in consuming countries and increase its real income and demand, with an increase – albeit delayed – in price. Conversely, when the dollar is strong and oil weak only the dollar area benefits from the lower cost of energy because in other importing countries they are compensated – at least in part – by the currency exchange, in which pricing is made. This example demonstrates the utility, in terms of transaction costs, stability and fairness of pricing in SDRs.[59]

Decisions that can extend the areas of use of the SDR as a unit of account are not up to the IMF (which already uses it) and therefore cannot be blocked by one or more countries that might be opposed to such a move. Individual users (institutions, banks, associations) will have to approve their use in accounting, financial statistics or the prices of raw materials. As regards oil, the decision could be taken by the OPEC or at least by those countries whose currency is officially pegged to the SDR. Libya has been one of these countries since 1986, when it stopped pegging its currency to the dollar.[60] Other African countries might find this solution convenient in light of the massive development plans announced by Europe (Mediterranean) and China (Indian Ocean). India is another country destined to increasingly influence the growth of African countries on the Indian Ocean and the importance of its currency could increase more quickly than expected in trade thus acquiring the other characteristics required for participation in the SDR basket.

Of the international reserve assets, the Fund itself underscores the unique nature of the *official SDR (O-SDR)* because of two of its distinguishing features: 1) it does not accumulate through balance of payments surplus but is allocated on the basis of IMF quotas; 2) it is not a liability for any specific economy but represents the potential right to obtain freely usable currencies for IMF members in other countries.[61] Holdings and transactions in SDRs are limited to participants in the SDR Department of the IMF and other prescribed holders (some international financial

[59] Elena Flor, "Un barile senza dollaro. Greggio, grano, monete: quanto pesa la speculazione", in *Il Sole 24 Ore* of 7 June 2017.

[60] Central Bank of Libya, *Exchange Rate Policy*, see: https://cbl.gov.ly/en/exchange-rate-policy/.

[61] IMF, Staff Notes for the G20, *op. cit.*, pp. 14-15.

institutions and central banks). The latter may hold SDRs but do not receive allocations.

The O-SDR carries an interest rate determined by the yields on the three-month treasury bills of the five countries issuing its component currencies, according to their weights, making its return comparable to that of other assets of the highest credit quality. The only interest-bearing SDRs are those that exceed the allocation to a country, representing its credit towards the others. Interests relating to SDRs received in allocation, however, are given to the Fund to finance mechanism costs.

Although the Second Amendment to the Articles of Agreement contains a commitment to making the O-SDR "the principal reserve asset of the IMS", its importance is still marginal because the necessary consensus has not been achieved on the reform proposals so far formulated. Significant reserve accumulation over the last two decades (after the 1997 Asian crisis and the 2007 global crisis), and the growing indebtedness of some reserve currency issuers, have again sparked discussion on the possible strengthening of the O-SDR's role as a reserve asset.

Some minimise concern over the imbalances in the balance of payments and the growth of precautionary currency reserves. Others (especially the governments of emerging and developing countries) are increasingly concerned about the outcome of the current "non-system" and are calling for its reform to correspond to the objective set out in the Second Amendment, i.e. to completely replace national currencies with an international currency as a reserve between different currency areas.

We have already seen how RTI has contributed to this debate on the side of those (such as Ocampo, Rajan, Stiglitz and Zhou) who believe that the O-SDR is able to mitigate the effects of the modern form of "the Triffin dilemma" and promote more effective collaboration between the IMF and central banks. This line of thinking is well summarised by the IMF Staff:

> According to this view, with the large magnitude and volatility of capital flows, and no mechanism for symmetric adjustment of surplus and deficit countries, the incentives are in place for: (i) excessive reserve accumulation and uphill capital flows as non-reserve-issuing countries attempt to avoid balance of payments deficits and build precautionary liquidity buffers; and (ii) undermining policy discipline in reserve currency issuers, manifested in current account and/or fiscal deficits. In such an environment external balances can become unanchored from fundamentals, or disinflationary pressures can emerge as all countries cannot simultaneously improve their balance of

payments. The O-SDR could help reduce these incentives by providing access to international liquidity.[62]

New SDR allocations and amendments to the Articles of Agreement are required to move towards the objective suggested by Triffin and as codified in the second amendment. The IMF's work, started by Dominique Strauss-Kahn and continued by Christine Lagarde, must not be interrupted in order to prepare for the change in the monetary regime which, if implemented, would mark *tout court* the end of hegemonies and the beginning of cooperative and controlled globalisation.

In the meantime, it would be useful to preserve the alternative monetary system set up by BRICS as an active and credible deterrent. When the US Congress was still determined to block the quota review in the Fund and the inclusion of the renminbi in the SDR basket, BRICS (Brazil Russia, India, China and South Africa), after signing a series of bilateral and multilateral agreements aimed at completely eliminating the use of the dollar in transactions between them, met in Fortaleza on 15 July 2014 to launch two new financial institutions. The first, the New Development Bank (NDB), based in Shanghai and whose first president was from India, was added to a number of regional or national development banks, whose total lending in 2013 exceeded the 52.6 billion issued by the World Bank. The NDB's capital, initially 50 billion dollars, could increase to 100 billion. The other institution, the Contingency Reserve Arrangement (CRA), is not a fund, but is a mechanism: a set of bilateral promises to provide currency reserves to countries in need. The following reserves have been guaranteed: $41 bn from China, $18 bn each from Brazil, Russia and India and $5 bn from South Africa. China is involved in another similar mechanism in agreement with some ASEAN countries. In addition, in 2013 China once again promoted the establishment of the Asian Infrastructure Investment Bank (AIIB). The AIIB will also play a major role in assembling the long-term financing needed for the construction of the "Silk Road". Among its founders are France, Germany, Italy and the UK.

To prepare the O-SDR playing field, the *SDR financial instruments market (M-SDR)* needs to be created and developed. Work can start immediately, following the example set by the World Bank with the issue in China.

Earlier, we saw how initial, premature attempts at creating this market gave no results (1975-85) and how the European basket market, the ECU,

---

[62]   IMF, Staff Notes for the G20, *op. cit.*, pp. 14-15.

was instead successfully created, leading to the establishment of the single currency (1978-1999). We have also touched on some of the causes that explain why instruments in SDR and in ECU were received differently by the markets. Returning to this point will help us answer the unavoidable question at the conclusion of this work: why something attempted 30-40 years ago is now more likely to succeed?

The first thing we must consider is the existence or the possibility of cultivating *political will*. The decision to create the *European Monetary System* and the ECU (1978) impressed markets by demonstrating governments' willingness to move towards closer regional integration policy. Instead, when looking at the case of the SDR, it was clear that the US was hostile to extending its use as an international currency. By the late 1980s, basing their reasoning on the different outcomes of the two baskets, most attentive observers pointed out the discrepancy between the great expectations placed in the SDR and its modest allocations, attributing the cause of this to political opposition: European opposition to promote the ECU outside the region, and US opposition to block the establishment of the SDR as the world's reserve currency.[63] At that point it was the SDR's universal scope that doomed it to clash with the still dominant US reason of state.

The current situation may seem challenging, if we only look at the US's attitude towards multilateral institutions, but it is far more balanced as to the distribution of power in the world. Today the convergence of the reasons of state of many large regional areas and countries representing the majority of the world economy is moving towards the defence of open trade by means of cooperative policies.

The United States, in particular, must make the most difficult choice in its history, and it is easy to understand why it cannot make up its mind between two opposing policies. The "Obama line" accepted this reality, as evidenced by the recognition of China's monetary and financial weight, and advocated a historical view of the exceptional conditions that enabled the US, after the Second World War, to set an example and drive the advancement of democracy and federalism in the world. In this way, it safeguards the ideals and moral heritage that have formed the acceptable face of American hegemony, making it a strong rationale for its constructive participation in world government, with the weight it deserves and respecting the reasons of others. Supranational organisations are essential to tackle global emergencies and to overcome nation states' crises, even

---

[63]   Philippe Jurgensen, *ECU. Naissance d'une monnaie*, Paris, J.C. Lattès, 1991.

fiscal crises, preventing them from responding to new security needs, sustainable development and equity, and being perceived by the public as a political crisis. However, attempts to dismantle the constraints of international cooperation are doomed to failure.

In addition to Europe and China, India, Latin America and Africa have also already expressed, although not all to the same degree in terms of preparedness and territorial extent, their will and ability to collaborate in the construction of regional monetary arrangements and participate in an international system organised in large areas, all pegged to the SDR, i.e. to themselves, to the value of their current production and potential. Countries that are not part of one of the existing areas will create new ones or use the SDR directly for their monetary and international finance needs.

Another ECU success factor, in part derived from the first, was the possibility that it offered, particularly to Belgium and Italy, to improve *access* to the international financial *market*. Investors, unwilling to commit capital in Belgian francs or Italian lira, judged the debt of public and private issuers from these countries less harshly when it was denominated in ECU. In addition to the normal benefits in exchange risks that a basket of currencies offers compared to a single state's currency, the ECU was also considered capable of reducing issuing risk, thanks to internal regulations required by the EMS for the individual states participating in it, with the aim of convergence.

At this stage, which issuers would be interested in debt securities in SDR, and for what reasons? Which other issuers would buy them, and why?

In the short term, the most likely potential issuers would be multilateral banks, regional development banks, governments and other public bodies, as well as multinational corporations. Countries with savings surpluses over domestic investments find it more convenient and safer to invest in emerging and developing countries, in renewable energy and global public goods, rather than – as they have hitherto done – in financing US consumption. This strategy corresponds perfectly to the logic of demographic curves because countries with a savings surplus (hence exports) are those with the oldest populations, that consume less and invest more to provide the returns necessary to support increased pension and health care spending. Emerging and developing countries, which have difficulty accessing capital markets, are the most dependent on the IMF and other supranational institutions. They often receive funding from the Fund in SDRs and, thanks to this support, can access financial markets more easily.

Other development factors for loans in SDR can also be assumed. One example involves two parties, the EIB and Libya. The development plan for Africa, which has started to shift from the decision-making level to the economic and financial level, will involve significant investment. A bank like the EIB undoubtedly contributes to compiling funding packages. For a country like Libya, whose dinar is pegged to the SDR, it would be convenient to receive loans in SDR because the revenues used to service its debt (from the sale of energy) will also be pegged to the SDR. If the EIB lends to Libya in SDR it will balance its position by financing itself through the issuance of bonds on the market in SDR. Other oil-producing countries may follow the example of Libya. In addition, public issuers will be able to recognise the intrinsic value of issuing instruments in SDRs and thus help create the M-SDR market, which will facilitate the subsequent issuance of O-SDRs. The more the M-SDR replaces dollar-denominated instruments, the sooner the US will find it necessary and/or convenient to borrow in SDRs, as they did at the time of the Bretton Woods crisis with *Roosa* Bonds, in European currencies.

When evaluating the potential demand for M-SDRs, it may be reasonably assumed this will come from investors responsible for large, diversified and long-term stability oriented investments. Now SDRs are also profitable because there are currencies with higher interest rates than the dollar in the basket. Insurance companies, pension funds and the like should always have a portion of their portfolio in M-SDR.

Like the ECU, the market will be successful once the M-SDR quotation is independent from the other component currencies in the basket, instead of being a result of their weighted average.

Finally, there are several *technical features* – or rather, "technical" features – because, like currency, as well as defence, even "technical features" are of great political significance. The concept of sovereignty is still closely associated with the *exclusively* sovereign power to issue currency and take up arms. Establishing, organising and defending national markets has been useful, but today is often an annoying "throwback" and hinders the constitutionalisation of international law. We are considering a method that is the most essential to creating a market: *clearing*, i.e. the compensation system. Tommaso Padoa-Schioppa defines it as follows:

> A set of infrastructure, technical-operational procedures and legal standards that allow participants to exchange and compensate for each other's claims for debit and credit, only settling final balances at the end of the clearing cycle. Balances can be calculated on a bilateral basis (i.e. in relation to each counterparty) or on a multilateral basis (in relation to the system as a whole).

Compensation systems may include both monetary payments and transactions in securities. International clearing systems (also referred to as "netting systems") are characterised by the management of payments or securities denominated in currencies other than the national one.[64]

The typical function of banking (the payment system) can create true credit when the bank responsible for compensation (in national systems, the central bank) finances imbalances arising from the clearing cycle. This financing can last a very short time, or even longer, up to 2-3 years. In the second case the bank gives the party with the outstanding balance the time to take the necessary measures to close their positions. In the case of the euro, whose creation was overseen by Tommaso Padoa-Schioppa himself, the system is called TARGET.[65] During crises, when there are asymmetric shocks, there tend to be payment imbalances between countries, and the ECB finances the corresponding demand for liquidity. It is well known that at certain times, TARGET has reflected German's high surplus (with respect to the ECB) and other countries' liabilities, including Italy. Without the liquidity provided by the ECB through TARGET, speculative attacks against the sovereign debt of some European countries would probably have triggered the destruction of the European monetary union and the EU itself.

Arguably, TARGET *is* the difference between the crisis of 1929 and that of 2007. In 1929 nobody listened to the enlightened economists and bankers, *clearing* failed and Germany was not given any "time" to repay. As there cannot be any "ifs" in the recording of history, we will never know whether the Weimar Republic would have spent that time wisely and whether Germany and the world would have thus been spared the horrors of Nazism.

In 1903 Paul Warburg wrote a booklet, *Plan for a Central Bank*, which, in the summer of 1913, and at the instigation of President Woodrow Wilson, laid the foundation for a vote to create twelve regional Reserve Banks and a Federal Reserve Bank in Washington: the Federal Reserve System, a central bank like the one in Germany. However, it took much longer to come up with the idea of a multilateral centralised clearing of credits and debts in the US. Warburg thought it inappropriate to assume

---

[64] Tommaso Padoa-Schioppa, *La moneta e il sistema dei pagamenti*, Bologna, il Mulino, 1992, p. 287 (the translation is ours).

[65] Trans-European Automated Real-Time Gross Settlement Express Transfer, now TARGET II, following some changes. It shares many similarities with the Fed system, the ISA (Interdistrict Settlement Accounts), which operates in the US.

chairmanship of the Fed because he had not been an American citizen long enough and was appointed its vice-president.

Warburg, Melchior[66] and Keynes opposed the reparations imposed on Germany by the Versailles Treaty. Warburg launched the idea of a bank specialised in the financing of reparations and in the revival of international trade. Only in 1929 was Warburg's International Acceptance Bank taken as a model for the creation of the Bank for International Settlements, after the restructuring of the German debt agreed by Young[67] and Schacht,[68] despite Adolf Hitler's vehement opposition. The BIS studied and implemented a true clearing system, but Hitler's rise to power, including debt repudiation, transformed its original purpose. With the creation of the Bank for International Settlements – BIS, many realised that Warburg's true goal (and then that of Keynes at Bretton Woods) was to create a World Bank. For example – as Jacques Attali recalls – Jacques Rueff, a young French finance inspector who at the time was unknown, declared at a conference in Paris:

"The Bank [BIS] prevents the governments concerned from guaranteeing the necessary foreign payments and maintaining to this end the various treasuries in foreign currency duplicating those of the issuing banks, established specifically for this purpose… This leads to the notion of a real 'currency BIS', freely convertible into other currencies at their exchange rates. If this road were pursued – as if in a dream – one could imagine a time when the credit bases of central banks were made only using gold and the indeterminate BIS currency. *Hence, there would truly be an international currency*". Illusion of reason [Attali concludes] swept away like the others in the maelstrom of the crisis.[69]

---

[66] At the Peace Conference, Melchior was part of the German delegation, as Keynes was part of the British delegation. He was later vice president of the BIS.

[67] Owen D. Young, American founder of Radio Corporation of America Industrial, chaired the committee that in 1929 restructured the unsustainable war debt left to Germany under the Treaty of Peace signed at Versailles in 1919.

[68] Hyalmar Schacht was appointed chief economist of the Weimar Republic in 1923 and in 1924 President of the German central bank, the Reichsbank, and participated in the drafting of the Young Plan. After Hitler's rise to power he was appointed Minister of Economy and returned as the chairman of the Reichsbank but resigned in 1937 because of critical, massive military spending. He was imprisoned after a failed attempt on Hitler's life and was declared "not guilty" at the Nuremberg trials against Nazi leaders.

[69] Jacques Attali, *Un homme d'influence. Sir Siegmund Warburg 1902-1982*, Paris, Fayard, 1985 (Biography of another family member, Siegmund, who after the Second World War rebuilt the Bank in London).

Keynes' bancor (with its *clearing*), Warburg's "BIS currency" – feared by Rueff who loved gold because France held it –, Triffin's SDR and the Second Amendment could be fully implemented now that the multi-currency international monetary system needs a common peg.

The IMF is the political driver of the SDR (through the key role of Ministers of Finance) while the BIS could be given the technical function of organising the compensation system (with a key role of Central Bank Governors). When this process will be completed, the three SDRs (unit of account, M-SDR and O-SDR) will be one and the same: the international currency.

CHAPTER 9

SDR: The Virtual Currency of the Future?

Christine Lagarde, Managing Director of the International Monetary Fund, in a speech in September 2017 to mark 20 years independence of the Bank of England, was questioned whether virtual currencies – such as the bitcoin – would pose any challenges to the current system of currencies and central banks.

Her answer was that, for the moment, it will not, because virtual currencies are "too volatile, too risky […] many are opaque […] and some have been hacked." However, there is a "growing demand for new payment services" for economies "rooted in peer-to-peer transactions, in frequent small-value payments, often across borders": in these cases, virtual currencies can be competitive compared to traditional systems such as credit cards.[70]

In the world of "big data", with new and more sophisticated technologies to interpret and use them, new financial intermediation models will emerge in the future: we are witnessing today their increasing use in the fields of consumer credit and mortgages.

The bitcoin and other virtual currencies will encounter problems and difficulties already well known to monetary history because, when faced with significant technological advantages – especially in the function as means of payment – the function as store of value may hold some bitter surprises for users who often will take – perhaps unwittingly – costly risks regarding their financial assets.

Gresham's law, according to which "bad money drives out good" – i.e. the holder tends to get rid of "bad money" and instead hoards "good money" – will also apply to virtual currencies. The challenge to systems subject to the supervision of regulators will therefore hardly be addressed by virtual currencies, which often leaves many victims in its wake.

---

[70] Christine Lagarde, "Central Banking and Fintech – A Brave New World?", Bank of England Conference, London, 29 September 2017 (see: https://www.imf.org/en/News/Articles/2017/09/28/sp092917-central-banking-and-fintech-a-brave-new-world).

In the payment system, the challenge is more open but, as noted by Christine Lagarde, some might have an interest in "hold[ing] virtual currency rather than dollars, euros [...] it may be easier and safer in the future than obtaining paper bills, especially in remote regions. And because virtual currencies could actually become more stable."[71]

However, there are conditions attached to the spread of these payment systems, the use of which would be a powerful incentive, especially at the international level: they must ensure the stability of the unit of account value in which they are expressed. There is only one way to achieve this: by pegging it to a currency or rather to a "stable currency basket". The link to gold or to other real assets would not solve the problem given their strong price fluctuations.

Sooner or later a virtual currency will peg to a currency or to a basket of currencies, which promises value, stability, and earn – again based on Gresham's law – a growing share of the market to the detriment of unstable virtual currencies.

The ability to operate internationally has always been typical of the emergence of new payment systems. This was the case with the emergence of wool merchants' letters of credit, which made Lyon a monetary centre in the 14th century, and with the credit card. The latter, introduced in the US in the 19th century as there was no federal banking system, and payments among different states were difficult because it was difficult to trust checks issued by other states' unknown banks (which perhaps did not even exist).

The virtual currency that will succeed in meeting this challenge will be the one that can carry out transactions, often international, for world citizens who are going to be buying more and more books, trips and smartphones using global chains, and which should therefore have price lists expressed in stable international units of account.

The "digital version of the SDR" is the ideal candidate; and the IMF – according to its General Manager – is open to collaboration.

---

[71] *Ibid.*

Annexes

A. Before Bretton Woods: The Keynes Plan*

The first draft of Lord Keynes' plan for a Clearing Union was circulated within the British Treasury on September 8, 1941.

A fourth draft was given to Ministers on February 11, 1942, and this is reproduced in (A) below.

The final draft was issued by the British Government in April 1943 as a White Paper (Cmd. 6437); it is reproduced in (B) below.

(A) Proposals for an International Currency
(or Clearing) Union
[February 11, 1942]

1. The proposal is to establish a Currency Union, here designated an International Clearing Union, based on international bank-money, called (let us say) bancor, fixed (but not unalterably) in terms of gold and accepted as the equivalent of gold by the British Commonwealth and the United States and all members of the Union for the purpose of settling international balances. The Central Banks of all member-States (and also of non-members) would keep accounts with the International Clearing Union through which they would be entitled to settle their exchange balances with one another at their par value as defined in terms of bancor. Countries having a favourable balance of payments with the rest of the world as a whole would find themselves in possession of a credit account with the Clearing Union, and those having an unfavourable balance would have a debit account. Measures would be necessary (see below) to prevent the piling up of credit and debit balances without limit, and the system would have failed in the long run if it did not possess sufficient capacity for self-equilibrium to prevent this.

2. The idea underlying such a Currency Union is simple, namely, to generalise the essential principle of banking, as it is exhibited within

---

* From *The International Monetary Fund 1945-1965 Twenty Years of International Monetary Cooperation* VOLUME III: DOCUMENTS Edited by J. Keith Horsefield, International Monetary Fund Washington, D. C., 1969

any closed system. This principle is the necessary equality of credits and debits, of assets and liabilities. If no credits can be removed outside the clearing system but only transferred within it, the Union itself can never be in difficulties. It can with safety make what advances it wishes to any of its members with the assurance that the proceeds can only be transferred to the clearing account of another member. Its problem is solely to see to it that its members keep the rules and that the advances made to each of them are prudent and advisable for the Union as a whole.

3. It is proposed that the Currency Union should be founded by the United States and the United Kingdom, which would be designated founder-States and given a special position. Their representatives, and those of other members, on the Governing Board of the Clearing Bank would be appointed by the Governments of the several member-States; the daily business and technical arrangements being carried out, as at present, by their Central Banks.

* * *

4. The plan aims at the substitution of an expansionist, in place of a contractionist, pressure on world trade.

5. It would effect this by allowing to each member-State overdraft facilities of a defined amount, proportionate to the importance of its foreign trade and subject to certain regulative provisions. That is to say, each country is allowed a certain margin of resources and a certain interval of time within which to effect a balance in its economic relations with the rest of the world. These facilities are made possible by the nature of the system itself and do not involve particular indebtedness between one member-State and another. A country is in credit or debit with the Clearing Union as a whole. This means that the overdraft facilities, whilst a relief to some, are not a real burden to others. For credit balances, just like the importation of actual gold, represent those resources which a country voluntarily chooses to leave idle. They represent a potentiality of purchasing power, which it is entitled to use at any time. Meanwhile, the fact that the creditor country is not choosing to employ this purchasing power would not necessarily mean, as it does at present, that it is withdrawn from circulation and exerting a deflationary and contractionist pressure on the whole world including the creditor country itself. No country need be in possession of a credit balance unless it deliberately prefers to sell more than it buys (or lends); no country loses its liquidity or is prevented from employing its credit balance whenever it chooses to do so; and no country suffers injury (but on the contrary) by the fact that the balance, which it does not choose to

employ for the time being, is not withdrawn from circulation. In short, the analogy with a national banking system is complete. No depositor in a local bank suffers because the balances, which he leaves idle, are employed to finance the business of someone else. Just as the development of national banking systems served to offset a deflationary pressure which would have prevented otherwise the development of modern industry, so by extending the same principle into the international field we may hope to offset the contractionist pressure which might otherwise overwhelm in social disorder and disappointment the good hopes of our modern world.

6. These facilities will be of particular importance as soon as the initial shortages of supply have been overcome. Many countries, including ourselves, will find a difficulty in paying for their imports, and will need time and resources before they can establish a readjustment. The efforts of each of these debtor countries to preserve its own equilibrium, by forcing its exports and by cutting off all imports which are not strictly necessary, will aggravate the problem of all the others. On the other hand, if each feels free from undue pressure, the volume of international exchange will be increased and everyone will find it easier to re-establish equilibrium without injury to the standard of life anywhere. The creditor countries will benefit, hardly less than the debtors, by being given an interval of time in which to adjust their economies, during which they can safely move at their own pace without the result of exercising deflationary pressure on the rest of the world, and, by repercussion, on themselves.

7. Now this can only be accomplished by the countries whoever they may turn out to be, which are for the time being in the creditor position, showing themselves ready to remain so without exercising a pressure towards contraction, pending the establishment of a new equilibrium. The fact that this costs them nothing deserves emphasising. The accumulation of a bancor credit, as compared with an accumulation of gold, does not curtail in the least their capacity or their inducement either to produce or to consume. The substitution of a credit mechanism for hoarding would have repeated in the international field the same miracle already performed in the domestic field of turning a stone into bread.

8. There might be one or two other ways of effecting this temporarily or in part. For example, U.S.A. might redistribute her gold. Or there might be a number of bilateral arrangements having the effect of providing international overdrafts, as for example an agreement by the Federal Reserve Board to accumulate, if necessary, a large sterling balance at the Bank of England.

9. The objection to particular arrangements of this kind is that they are likely to be influenced by extraneous, political reasons and put individual countries into a position of particular obligation towards others; and also that the distribution of the assistance between different countries may not correspond to need and to the actual requirements as they ultimately develop. Moreover, for reasons already given, we are not likely to be specially eligible applicants for bounty of this kind. If, for example, the problem were to be met by a redistribution of America's gold, it is unlikely that we should get any of it, partly because we should have so lately received assistance under Lend-Lease, partly because the British Commonwealth are the largest producers of gold, which output would be regarded, rightly or wrongly, as ours at one remove.

10. It should be much easier, and surely more satisfactory both for them and for us, to persuade the United States to enter into a general and collective responsibility, applying to all countries alike, that a country finding itself in a creditor position against the rest of the world as a whole should enter into an arrangement not to allow this credit balance so long as it chooses to hold it, to exercise a contractionist pressure against world economy and, by repercussion, against the economy of the creditor country itself. This would give us, and all others, the great assistance of multilateral clearing, whereby (for example) we could offset favourable balances arising out of our exports to Europe against unfavourable balances due to the United States or South America or elsewhere. How, indeed, can we hope to afford to start up trade with Europe (which will be of vast importance to us) during the relief and reconstruction period on any other terms?

11. These advantages of the proposed International Clearing Union are so great that they surely overshadow most reasons of objection on lesser grounds.

12. If, indeed, we lack the productive capacity to maintain our standard of life, then a reduction in this standard is not avoidable. If our wage and price-levels are hopelessly wrong, a change in the rate of exchange is inevitable. But if we possess the productive capacity and the difficulty is the lack of markets as a result of restrictive policies throughout the world, then the remedy lies in expanding opportunities for export by removal of restrictive pressure. There is great force in the contention that, if active employment and ample purchasing power can be sustained in the main centres of world trade, the problem of surpluses and unwanted exports will largely disappear, even though under the most prosperous conditions there may remain some disturbances of trade and unforeseen situations requiring special remedies.

13. There is no obvious means of offering a right measure of inducement to the general expansion of international trade except by a broadly based international organisation.

* * *

14. The arrangement by which the members of the Clearing Union start with substantial overdraft facilities in hand will be mainly useful, just as the possession of any kind of reserve is useful, to allow time and method for necessary adjustments and a comfortable safeguard behind which the unforeseen and the unexpected can be faced with equanimity. Obviously, it does not by itself provide any long-term solution against a continuing disequilibrium, for in due course the more improvident and the more impecunious, left to themselves, would have run through their resources. But, if the purpose of the overdraft facilities is mainly to give time for adjustments, we have to make sure, so far as possible, that they will be made. We must have, therefore, some rules and some machinery to provide that equilibrium is restored.

15. Perhaps the most difficult question to determine is how much to decide by rule and how much to leave to discretion. If rule prevails, the liabilities attaching to membership of the system are definite, whilst the responsibilities of central management are reduced to a minimum. On the other hand, liabilities which would require the surrender by legislation of too much of the discretion, normally inherent in a Government, will not be readily undertaken by ourselves or by the United States. If discretion prevails, how far can the ultimate decision be left to the individual members and how far to the central management? If the individual members are too free, indiscipline may result and unwarrantable liberties be taken. But if it is to the central management that the discretions are given, too heavy a weight of responsibility may rest on it, and it may be assuming the exercise of powers which it has not the strength to implement. If rule prevails, the scheme can be made more water-tight theoretically. But if discretion prevails, it may work better in practice. All this is the typical problem of any supernational authority. An earlier draft of this proposal was criticised for leaning too much to the side of rule. In the provisions below the bias is in the other direction. For it may be better not to attempt to settle too much beforehand and to provide that the plan shall be reconsidered after an initial experimental period of (say) five years. Only by collective wisdom and discussion can the right compromise be reached between law and licence.

16. The proposal put forward below differs in one important respect from the pre-war system because it aims at putting some part of the

responsibility for adjustment on the creditor country as well as on the debtor. This is an attempt to recover the advantages which were enjoyed in the 19th century when a favourable balance in favour of London and Paris, which were the main creditor centres, immediately produced an expansionist pressure in those markets, but which have been lost since New York succeeded to the position of main creditor, the effect of this change being aggravated by the breakdown of international borrowing credit and by the flight of loose funds from one depository to another. The object is that the creditor should not be allowed to remain entirely passive. For if he is, an intolerably heavy task may be laid on the debtor country, which is already for that very reason in the weaker position.

17. The detailed provisions proposed (the particular proportions, &c., suggested being merely tentative as a basis of discussion) are the following:

(1) The two founder States will agree between themselves the initial values of their own currencies in terms of bancor and the value of bancor in terms of gold; and the initial values of the currencies of other members will be fixed on their joining the system in agreement with them. A member-State may not subsequently alter the value of its currency in terms of bancor without the permission of the Governing Board except under the conditions dealt with below; but during the first five years after the inception of the system the Governing Board shall give special consideration to appeals for adjustments in the exchange-value of a national currency on the ground of unforeseen circumstances.

(2) The amount of the maximum debit balance allowed to any member-State shall be determined by reference to the amount of its foreign trade, and shall be designated its quota. There need be no limit to the amount of a credit balance.

The initial quotas might be fixed by reference to the sum of each country's exports and imports on the average of (say) the three pre-war years, being either equal or in a determined lesser proportion to this amount, a special assessment being substituted in cases where this formula would be, for any reason, inappropriate. Subsequently, after the elapse of the transitional period, the quotas might be revised annually in accordance with the actual volume of trade in the three preceding years.

(3) A charge of 1 per cent. per annum will be payable to the Reserve Fund of the Clearing Union on the average balance of a member-State, whether credit or debit, in excess of a quarter of its quota;

and a further charge of 1 per cent. on the average balance, whether credit or debit, in excess of half its quota. Thus only a country which keeps as nearly as possible in a state of international balance on the average of the year will escape this contribution. These particular charges are, clearly, not essential to the scheme. But if they are found acceptable, they would be valuable inducements towards keeping a level balance, and a significant indication that the System looks on excessive credit balances with as critical an eye as on excessive debit balances, each being, indeed, the inevitable concomitant of the other. Any member-State in debit may, however, borrow from the balances of any member-State in credit on such terms as may be mutually agreed, by which means each would avoid these contributions.

(4) *(a)* A member-State may not increase its debit balance by more than a quarter of its quota within a year without the permission of the Governing Board. If its debit balance has exceeded a quarter of its quota on the average of at least a year, it shall be entitled to reduce the value of its currency in terms of bancor, provided that the reduction shall not exceed 5 per cent. within a year without the permission of the Governing Board.

(b) As a condition of allowing a member-State to increase its debit balance in excess of a half of its quota, the Governing Board may require (i) a stated reduction in the value of the member's currency, if it deems that to be the suitable remedy, (ii) the control of outward capital transactions if not already in force, and (iii) the surrender of a suitable proportion of any separate gold reserve it may hold in reduction of its debit balance.

(c) If a member-State's debit balance has exceeded three-quarters of its quota on the average of at least a year [or is excessive, as measured by some formula laid down by the Governing Board, in relation to the total debit balances outstanding on the books of the Clearing Union], it may be asked by the Governing Board to take measures to improve its position and, in the event of its failing to reduce its debit balance below the figure in question within two years, the Governing Board may declare that it is in default and no longer entitled to draw against its account except with the permission of the Governing Board. Each member-State, on joining the system, shall agree to pay to the Clearing Union any payments due from it to a country in default towards the discharge of the latter's debit balance and to accept this arrangement in the event of falling into default itself. A member-State which resigns from the Clearing Union without making approved arrangements for the discharge of any debit balance shall also be treated as in default.

(5) A member-State whose credit balance has exceeded a half of its quota on the average of at least a year shall discuss with the Governing Board (but shall retain the ultimate decision in its own hands) what measures would be appropriate to restore the equilibrium of its international balances, including

(a) measures for the expansion of domestic credit and domestic demand;

(b) the appreciation of its local currency in terms of bancor, or, alternatively, an increase in money-wages;

(c) the reduction of excessive tariffs and other discouragements against imports;

(d) international loans for the development of backward countries.

* * *

18. The special protective expedients which were developed between the two wars were sometimes due to political, social or industrial reasons. But frequently they were nothing more than forced and undesired dodges to protect an unbalanced position of a country's overseas payments. The new system, by providing an automatic register of the size and whereabouts of the aggregate debtor and creditor positions respectively, will give a clear indication whether it is reasonable for a particular country to adopt special expedients as a temporary measure to assist in regaining equilibrium in its balance of payments, in spite of a general rule not to adopt them.

19. It is not proposed to incorporate any specific arrangements for such relaxations in the constitution of the Clearing Union itself. But the existence of the Clearing Union would make it possible for member States contracting Commercial Treaties to use their respective debit and credit positions with the Clearing Union as a test. Thus, the contracting parties, whilst agreeing to clauses in a Commercial Treaty forbidding, in general, the use of certain measures or expedients in their mutual trade relations, might make this agreement subject to special relaxations if the state of their respective clearing accounts satisfied an agreed criterion. For example, a Treaty might provide that, in the event of one of the contracting States having a debit balance with the Clearing Union exceeding a specified proportion of its quota on the average of a period and the other having a credit balance of a specified amount, the former should be free to resort to import quotas or to barter trade agreements or to higher import duties of a type which was not permitted under the Treaty in normal circumstances. It might even provide that such exceptions should only be allowed subject to the approval of the governing Board of the Clearing Union, and in that case the possible grounds for exceptional action might cover a wider field and other contingencies.

20. Apart from such temporary indulgence, the members of the Clearing Union should feel sufficiently free from anxiety to contemplate the ultimate removal of the more dislocating forms of protection and discrimination and expect the prohibition of some of the worst of them from the outset. In any case, members of the Currency Union would not allow or suffer among themselves any restrictions on the disposal of receipts arising out of current trade or "invisible" income. It might also be possible to obtain recognition of the general principle that commercial treaties between members of the Union should, subject to any necessary safeguards and exceptions, exclude

(i) import restrictions, whether quantitative or in the form of "duty-quotas" (excluding, however, prohibitions genuinely designed to safeguard, e.g., public health or morale or revenue collection);

(ii) barter arrangements;

(iii) export quotas and discriminatory export taxes;

(iv) export subsidies either furnished directly by the State or indirectly under schemes supported or encouraged by the State; and

(v) excessive tariffs.

21. Subsidies in favour of domestic producers for domestic consumption, with a countervailing levy when such subsidised goods are exported, would not be excluded. This is a necessary safety-valve which provides for protective expedients called for on political, social and industrial grounds. Such subsidies and tariffs would be a permitted way of giving purely domestic protection to an industry which for special reasons ought to be maintained for domestic purposes only. The question of preferences and of other relaxations from most-favoured-nation treatment, which would be of a normal and continuing character, does not fall within the scope of this paper, and must be settled on principles outside the sphere of the Clearing Union.

22. The above provisions might enable us to give some satisfaction to Mr. Cordell Hull over a wide field, since we should be accepting a non-discriminatory international system as the normal and desirable regime.

* * *

23. It is a great advantage of the proposed Currency Union that it restores unfettered multilateral clearing between its members; so that no action is necessary, except where a country is out of balance with the system as a whole.

24. Compare this with the difficulties and complications of a large number of bilateral agreements. Compare, above all, the provisions by which a country, taking improper advantage of a payments agreement (for the system is, in fact, a generalised payments agreement) as Germany did before the war, is dealt with not by a single country (which may not be strong enough to act effectively in isolation or cannot afford to incur the diplomatic odium of isolated action) but by the system as a whole.

If the argument is used that the Currency Union may have difficulty in disciplining a misbehaving country and in avoiding consequential loss, with what much greater force can we urge this objection against a multiplicity of separate bilateral payments agreements.

25. Thus we should not only return to the advantages of an international gold currency, but we might enjoy them more widely than was ever possible in practice with the old system under which at any given time only a minority of countries were actually working with free exchanges.

26. The advantages of multilateral clearing are of particular importance to London. It is not too much to say that this is an essential condition of the continued maintenance of London as the banking centre of the Sterling Area. Under a system of bilateral agreements it would seem inevitable that the sterling area, in the form in which it has been historically developed and as it has been understood and accepted by the Dominions and India, must fall to pieces.

27. In conditions of multilateral clearing everything would go on exactly as before without our having to ask anyone to accept special or onerous conditions. We should, in this respect, be back again in the best days of the gold standard. The traditional advantages of banking in London would be retained, precisely because London has been built up on the basis of an international currency having universal validity. But if we try to make of the sterling area a compact currency union as against the rest of the world, we shall be putting a greater strain on arrangements, which have been essentially (even in time of war) *informal*, than they can be expected to bear.

28. It is possible to combine countries, some of which will be in a debtor and some in a creditor position, into a Currency Union which, substantially, covers the world. But, surely, it is impossible, unless they have a common banking and economic system also, to combine them into a Currency Union not with, but against, the world as a whole. If other members of the sterling area have a favourable balance against the world as a whole, they will lose nothing by keeping them in sterling, which will be interchangeable with bancor and hence with any other currency, until they have occasion to use them. But if the sterling area is turned into a Currency Union, the members

in credit would have to make a forced and *non-liquid* loan of their favourable balances to the members in debit. Incidentally, they might find themselves involved in making between them an involuntary loan to London at the rate, perhaps, of £100,000,000 a year cumulative. They would have to impose import regulations and restraints on capital movements according as the area as a whole was in debit or credit, irrespective of their own positions. They would have to be bound by numerous bilateral agreements negotiated primarily (at least so they would believe) in the interests of London. The sterling resources of creditor Dominions might come to be represented by nothing but blocked balances in a number of doubtfully solvent countries with whom it suited us to trade. Moreover, it is difficult to see how the system could work without a pooling of gold reserves.

29. It is improbable that South Africa or India would accept such arrangements even if other Dominions were more complying. We should soon find ourselves, therefore, linked up only with those constituents which were running at a debit, apart from the Crown Colonies, which, perhaps, we could insist on keeping.

30. Is it not a delusion to suppose that the *de facto*, but somewhat flimsy and unsatisfactory, arrangements, which are carrying us through the war, on the basis that we do our best to find the other members of the area a limited amount of dollars provided that they lend us a very much larger sum in sterling, can be carried over into the peace and formalised into a working system based on a series of bilateral agreements with the rest of the world, accompanied by a strict control of capital movements outside the Area?

31. The sterling area, if we mean by this the system under which the members of the British Commonwealth do their international banking through London, grew up under conditions of freedom. It lives and breathes by being a voluntary system. It is only in that same atmosphere of the City of London as Liberty Hall dealing in a currency of general acceptability that we can expect to preserve it. The notion that a multilateral plan, based on an international standard, jeopardises the position of the Sterling Area must be based on a rigid and (one would think) politically impracticable version of the Sterling Area concept and not on its historical and actual significance.

A multilateral plan would, therefore, be of great assistance in maintaining the position of London in relation both to the British Commonwealth and to many other countries which like our way of doing business and would give up most reluctantly the facilities we have given them.

* * *

32. It may be convenient at this point to note in more detail the position contemplated for centres of international banking such as London, New York or Paris, and for currency groups within the membership of the Clearing Union covering more than one country, such as the existing sterling area or groups, like the Latin Union of former days, which may come into existence covering, for example, the countries of North America or those of South America or the groups now under active discussion covering Poland and Czechoslovakia or certain of the Balkan States.

33. The governing principles should be: first, that the Clearing Union is set up, not for the transaction of daily business between individual traders or banks, but for the clearing and settlement of the ultimate outstanding balances between Central Banks (and certain other super-national Institutions), such as would have been settled under the old gold standard by the shipment or the earmarking of gold, and should not trespass unnecessarily beyond this field; and, secondly, that its purpose is to increase freedom in international commerce and not to multiply interferences or compulsions.

34. Thus the fabric of international banking organisation, built up by long experience to satisfy practical needs, should be left as undisturbed as possible. Except as regards a provision, explained below, concerning the balances of Central Banks themselves, there should be no obstacle in the way of the existing practices of international banking except those which necessarily arise through measures which individual Central Banks may choose to adopt for the control of movements of capital.

35. Nor should it be necessary to interfere with the discretion of Central Banks which desire to maintain a special intimacy within a particular group of countries associated by geographical or political ties. There is no reason why such Central Banks should not be allowed a double position, both as members of the Clearing Union in their own right with their proper quota, and also as making use of another financial centre along traditional lines, as for example, Australia and India with London or certain American countries with New York. In this case their accounts with the Clearing Union would be in exactly the same position as the independent gold reserves which they now maintain, and they would have no occasion to modify in any way their present practices in the conduct of daily business.

36. There would be other cases, however, in which a dependency or a member of a federal union would merge its currency identity in that of a mother Central Bank, with a quota appropriate to the merged currency unit as a whole, and not enjoy a separate individual membership of the

Clearing Union, as, for example, the French colonies, the Federated States of the American Union or of Australia, and possibly the British Crown Colonies.

37. At the same time there should be a general encouragement to Central Banks, which do not belong to a special geographical or political group, to keep their reserve balances with the Clearing Union and not with one another, except in the case of a specific loan from a member-State in credit with the Clearing Union to a member-State in debit. It should, therefore, be laid down that overseas balances may not be held in another country except with the approval of the Central Bank of that country; and, in order that sterling and dollars might not appear to compete with bancor for the purpose of Central Bank reserve balances, the Founder States might agree together that they would not accept the reserve balances of other Central Banks in excess of normal working balances except in the case of Banks definitely belonging to a Sterling Area or Dollar Area group.

* * *

38. The position of gold would be left substantially unchanged. What, in the long run, the world may decide to do with gold is another matter. The establishment of an International Clearing Union does not require any significant or immediate change. Indeed, by providing an automatic means by which some part of the favourable balances of the creditor countries can be settled, the current gold production of the world and the remnant of gold reserves held outside the United States may yet have a useful part to play. Moreover, gold still possesses great psychological value which will not have been diminished by recent events; for the desire to possess a gold reserve against unforeseen contingencies is likely to remain. Gold also has the merit of providing, in point of form whatever the underlying realities may be, an uncontroversial standard of value for international purposes, for which it would not yet be easy to find a serviceable substitute.

39. It is conceived, therefore, that the international bank-money which we have designated *bancor* would be defined in terms of a weight of gold. Since the national currencies of the member-States would also be given a defined exchange value in terms of bancor, it follows that they would have a defined gold content which would also be their official buying price for gold above which they must not pay. Any Central Bank would be entitled to obtain a credit in terms of bancor by paying actual gold to the credit of its Clearing Account, thus securing a steady and ascertained purchaser for the output of the gold-producing countries and for countries holding a large reserve of gold.

40. Central Banks would be entitled to retain their separate gold reserves and ship gold to one another against a clearance between them in the books of the Clearing Union, provided they did not pay a price above parity; they could coin gold and put it into circulation, and, generally speaking, do what they liked with it.

41. One restriction only would be, for obvious reasons, essential. No Central Bank would be entitled to demand gold from the Clearing Union against its balance of bancor; for bancor would be available only for transfer to the Clearing Account of another Central Bank. Thus between gold and bancor itself there would be a one-way convertibility only, such as ruled frequently before the war with national currencies which were on what was usually called a "gold-exchange standard." This need not mean that the Clearing Union would only receive gold and never pay it out. If the Clearing Union found itself in possession of a stock of gold, the Governors of the Bank should have the discretion to distribute the surplus between all Central Banks possessing a credit balance with it, proportionately to such balances, in reduction of their amount.

42. The question has been raised whether these arrangements are compatible with the retention by individual member-States of a full gold standard with two-way convertibility, so that, for example, any foreign bank acquiring dollars through the Clearing Union could use them to obtain gold for export. It is not evident that a good purpose would be served by this. But if any member-State should prefer to maintain full convertibility for internal purposes, it could protect itself from any abuse of the system or inconvenient consequences by providing that gold could only be exported under licence.

43. The value of bancor in terms of gold should be fixed but not unalterably. The two founder States, the United States and the United Kingdom, acting in agreement, should have the power to change it. Clearly, they should exercise this power if the stocks of gold tendered to the bank were to be super-abundant for their legitimate purposes. No object would be served by attempting further to peer into the future or to prophesy the ultimate policy of the founder States in this regard.

44. Changes in the value of the national currencies of member-States stand in a different category. For the real significance of such changes is to be found not in relation to gold itself but in relation to the values of national currencies amongst themselves. The general principles by which such changes should be governed have been discussed in a previous section. It would be undesirable, if it can be avoided, to lay down more precise rules in advance, since it is difficult to distinguish by means of

a rigid formula the cases, in which a change in the rate of exchange will assist the restoration of equilibrium and is the right remedy, from those cases where some other type of measure is more appropriate.

* * *

45. It is widely held that control of capital movements, both inward and outward, should be a permanent feature of the post-war system – at least so far as we are concerned. If control is to be effective, it probably involves the machinery of exchange control for all transactions, even though a general open licence is given to all remittances in respect of current trade. But such control will be more difficult to work, especially in the absence of a postal censorship, by unilateral action than if movements of capital can be controlled *at both ends*. It would therefore be of great advantage if the United States and all other members of the Currency Union would adopt machinery similar to that which we have now gone a long way towards perfecting in this country; though this cannot be regarded as *essential* to the proposed Union.

46. This does not mean that the era of international investment should be brought to an end. On the contrary, the system contemplated should greatly facilitate the restoration of international credit for loan purposes in ways to be discussed below. The object, and it is a vital object, is to have a means of distinguishing

(*a*) between movements of floating funds and genuine new investment for developing the world's resources; and

(*b*) between movements, which will help to maintain equilibrium, from surplus countries to deficiency countries and speculative movements or flights out of deficiency countries or from one surplus country to another.

47. There is no country which can, in future, safely allow the flight of funds for political reasons or to evade domestic taxation or in anticipation of the owner turning refugee. Equally, there is no country that can safely receive fugitive funds which cannot safely be used for fixed investment and might turn it into a surplus country against its will and contrary to the real facts.

48. The general principles of the control of capital movements need not be discussed here. It is evident that the existence of an International Clearing Union would make such control easier.

* * *

49. It has been suggested that so ambitious a proposal is open to criticism on the ground that it requires from the members of the Currency Union a greater surrender of their sovereign rights than they will readily concede.

50. But, in the present version of the plan, no greater surrender is required than in any commercial treaty – certainly not greater than in the binding undertakings against discrimination which the United States is inviting us to make. The obligations will be entered into voluntarily and can be terminated on certain conditions by giving notice.

51. In the second place a greater readiness to accept super-national arrangements must be required in the post-war world than hitherto. The arrangements proposed could be described as a measure of Financial Disarmament. They are very mild in comparison with the measures of Military Disarmament, which it is to be hoped the world may be asked to accept.

52. Surely it is an advantage, rather than a disadvantage, of the scheme that it invites the member States and groups to abandon that licence to promote indiscipline, disorder and bad-neighbourliness which, to the general disadvantage, they have been free to exercise hitherto.

53. There is nothing here which we need be reluctant to accept ourselves or to ask of others. Or if there be anything such, let it be amended.

* * *

54. An International Currency Union might become the instrument and the support of international policies apart from those which it is its primary purpose to promote. The following suggestions are not a necessary part of the plan. But they are illustrations of the additional purposes of high importance and value which the Union, once established, might be able to serve:

(1) The Union might set up a clearing account in favour of the international body charged with post-war Relief and Reconstruction. If necessary, it might supplement contributions received from other sources by granting overdraft facilities in favour of this body, this overdraft being discharged over a period of years out of the Reserve Fund of the Union, or, if necessary, out of a levy on credit clearing balances. By this means it is possible to avoid asking any country to assume a burdensome commitment for relief and reconstruction, since the resources would be provided in the first instance by those countries having credit Clearing Accounts for which they have no immediate use and are voluntarily leaving idle, and in the long run

by those countries which have a chronic international surplus for which they have no beneficial employment.

(2) If the United States were to wish to effect a redistribution of gold reserves, the Clearing Union would provide a suitable channel for the purpose, the gold so re-distributed being credited (e.g.) to the account of the Relief and Reconstruction Authority.

(3) The Union might set up an account in favour of the Super-national policing body charged with the duty of preserving the peace and maintaining international order. If any country were to infringe its properly authorised orders, the policing body might be entitled to request the Governors of the Clearing Union to hold the Clearing Account of the Central Bank of the delinquent country to its order and permit no further transactions on the account except by its authority. This would provide an excellent machinery for enforcing a financial blockade.

(4) The Union might set up an account in favour of international bodies charged with the management of a Commodity Control, and might finance stocks of commodities held by such bodies, allowing them overdraft facilities on their accounts up to an agreed maximum. By this means the financial problem of holding pools and "evernormal granaries" would be satisfactorily solved.

(5) The Union might be closely linked up with the Board for International Investment. It might act on behalf of this Board and collect for them the annual service of their loans by automatically debiting the Clearing Account of the country concerned. The statistics of the Clearing Accounts of the Member States would give a reliable indication as to which countries were in a position to finance the Investment Board, with the advantage of shifting the whole system of clearing credits and debits nearer to equilibrium. This important question is the subject of a separate paper.

(6) There are various methods by which the Clearing Union could use its influence and its powers to maintain stability of prices and to control the Trade Cycle. If an International Economic Board is established, this Board and the Clearing Union might be expected to work in close collaboration to their mutual great advantage. If an International Investment or Development Corporation is also set up together with a scheme of Commodity Boards for the control of stocks of the staple raw materials, we might come to possess in these four Institutions a powerful means of combating the evils of the Trade Cycle, by exercising contractionist or expansionist influence

on the system as a whole or on particular sections. This, again, is a large and important question which cannot be discussed adequately in this paper; and need not be examined at length in this place because it does not raise any important issues affecting the fundamental constitution of the proposed Union. It is mentioned here to complete the picture of the large purposes which the foundation of the Currency Union might be made to serve.

* * *

55. Our post-war currency and exchange system should be one which is capable of wide, indeed of universal, extension as further countries become ready for it. Nevertheless it would be an advantage if the proposed Union could be brought into existence by the United States and the United Kingdom as joint founder-States, covering the United States and its possessions and the members of the British Commonwealth. The position of Russia, which might be a third founder, if she can be a party to so capitalist-looking an institution, would need special consideration. Other members would then be brought in – some from the outset, some as soon as they had established an internal organisation capable of sustaining the obligations of membership. This approach would have the great advantage that the United States and the United Kingdom (the former in consultation with the Pan-American countries and the latter with the other members of the British Commonwealth) could settle the charter and the main details of the new body without being subjected to the delays and confused counsels of an international conference. It would also mean that considerable progress could be made irrespective of the nature of the European political settlement and before the conditions of adherence of the European members could be finally determined. Moreover, membership would be thus established as a privilege only open to those who conformed to certain general principles and standards of international economic conduct. The management and the effective voting power might inhere permanently in the founder-States.

56. In view of our experience and of our geographical and political position in relation to Europe, the United States and the British Commonwealth, we could justifiably ask that the head office should be situated in London with the Board of Managers meeting alternately here and in Washington.

57. Members of the Board would be appointed by the Governments of the member-States, each of which would have a vote in proportion to its quota. But there might be a provision, at any rate for the first five years,

by which the British and American members when acting in agreement could outvote the rest of the Board.

58. There is no reason why the Central Banks of non-member States should not keep Credit Clearing Accounts with the Union; and indeed it would be advisable for them to do so for the conduct of their trade with member-States. But they would have no say in the management.

59. Members should be entitled to withdraw from the Union on a year's notice, subject to their making satisfactory arrangements to discharge any debit balance. They would not, of course, be able to employ any credit balance except by making transfers from it, either before or after their withdrawal, to the Clearing Accounts of other Central Banks. Similarly it should be within the power of the Governing Board to require the withdrawal of a member subject to the same notice.

60. The principles and governing rules of the Union should be the subject of general reconsideration after five years' experience, if a majority of the Governing Board desire it.

61. It would be of great advantage if the general principles of the International Clearing Union could be agreed beforehand, with a view to bringing it into operation at an early date after the termination of hostilities. Such a proposal presents, however, something of a dilemma. On the one hand, many countries, ourselves not least, will be in particular need of reserves of overseas resources in the period immediately after the war. On the other hand, goods will be in short supply and the prevention of inflationary international conditions of the first importance. The expansionist tendency of the proposed system, which is a leading recommendation of it as soon as peace-time output is restored and the productive capacity of the world is in running order, might easily be a danger in the early days of a sellers' market and a superabundance of demand over supply.

62. A reconciliation in detail of these divergent purposes is not easily found until we know more than is known at present about the means to be adopted to finance post-war relief and reconstruction and particularly as to the intentions of the United States regarding a temporary continuance of Lease-Lend arrangements for food and raw materials after the termination of hostilities. If these intentions are on liberal and comprehensive lines, it might be better for relief and Lend-Lease arrangements to take the place of the proposed quotas during the "relief" period of (say) two years. The immediate establishment of the Clearing Union would be compatible with provisional arrangements regarding the overdraft quotas which could take alternative forms according to the character of the other "relief" arrangements.

63. If the finance of relief is actually furnished through the Clearing Union, which has been suggested above as one possibility, and if that, combined with some continuance of lend-leasing by the United States, appears likely to provide the world with as much purchasing power as is desirable in the early days, the coming into force of the overdraft quotas might be postponed until the Founder Members are agreed that the need for them is impending. In this case credit clearing balances would be limited to the amount of gold delivered to the Union, and the overdraft facilities created by the Union in favour of the Relief Council, the International Investment Board or the Commodity Controls. Alternatively overdraft quotas might be allowed on a reduced scale during the transitional period. At any rate, it might be proper to provide that countries in receipt of relief or Lend-Lease assistance should not have access at the same time to overdraft facilities, and that the latter should only become available when the former had come to an end.

64. If, on the other hand, relief and Lend-Lease facilities look like being inadequate from the outset, the overdraft quotas may be even more necessary at the outset than later on.

65. We must not be over-cautious. A rapid economic restoration may lighten the tasks of the diplomatists and the politicians in the resettlement of the world and the restoration of social order. In our case the possibility of exports sufficiently expanded to sustain our standard of life and our solvency is bound up with good and expanding markets. We cannot afford to wait too long for this and we must not allow excessive caution to condemn us to perdition. Unless the Union is a going concern, the problem of proper "timing" will be almost insoluble. It is sufficient at this stage to point out that the problem of timing must not be overlooked, but that the Union is capable of being used so as to aid rather than impede its solution.

* * *

66. In most of its objectives and in many of its methods this paper is in fundamental accord with alternative proposals which have been or could be put forward.

The special merits claimed for this particular version include the following:

For ourselves.

(1) Our British problem of gaining enough receipts overseas to balance our import requirements is so acute that we can scarcely hope to solve it except through a scheme which

(a) by a strong expansionist stimulus throughout the world provides willing markets for a largely expanded volume of our exports;

(b) offers facilities for the multilateral clearing of international payments, since we cannot afford to have any of the credit balances, which we may acquire overseas, to be blocked and unavailable as a set-off against our debit balances elsewhere;

(c) provides us with a margin, during the period before we can re-establish equilibrium, by an international scheme which does not require us to ask particular favours or accommodations from the United States but merely gives to us, and requires of us, the same facilities for the expansion of international trade and the maintenance of international equilibrium which all the countries will be asked to receive and to allow;

(d) affords us the possibility of subsequent rectifications of the rate of exchange against the rest of the world without the risk of competitive depreciations or of complaints by other countries in the event of the initial value of sterling proving to be higher than the level at which we can balance our overseas trade.

(2) A multilateral system preserves, to the full extent compatible with the control of capital movements, the traditional freedom of London as a financial centre. Above all it allows the historical continuity of the sterling area in the same form and with the same absence of restraint as heretofore. For it is evident that any system of numerous bilateral agreements would put in great jeopardy not only the sterling area but the whole position of London as an international centre.

For the United States and the World at large.

(1) It provides a general framework by the aid of which all countries can hope to rehabilitate their currencies.

(2) It offers a criterion by the help of which we can satisfy American aspirations, which we ourselves share with Mr. Hull and Mr. Sumner Welles, for the greater freedom of international trade supported by firm undertakings.

(3) It is a plan which can be used to further such general world purposes as

(a) post-war relief and reconstruction;

(b) international T.V.A.;

(c) the finance of commodity agreements;

(d) the preservation of peace;

(e) the control of the Trade Cycle and the stabilisation of prices; and, generally,

(f) the maintenance of active employment everywhere.

(4) It is capable of arousing enthusiasm because it makes a beginning at the future economic ordering of the world between nations and "the winning of the peace," and might help to create the conditions and the atmosphere in which much else would be made easier.

(B) Proposals for an International Clearing Union[72]
(April 1943)
PREFACE

Immediately after the war all countries who have been engaged will be concerned with the pressure of relief and urgent reconstruction. The transition out of this into the normal world of the future cannot be wisely effected unless we know into what we are moving. It is therefore not too soon to consider what is to come after. In the field of national activity occupied by production, trade and finance, both the nature of the problem and the experience of the period between the wars suggest four main lines of approach:

1. The mechanism of currency and exchange;

2. The framework of a commercial policy regulating the conditions for the exchange of goods, tariffs, preferences, subsidies, import regulations and the like;

3. The orderly conduct of production, distribution and price of primary products so as to protect both producers and consumers from the loss and risk for which the extravagant fluctuations of market conditions have been responsible in recent times;

4. Investment aid, both medium and long term, for the countries whose economic development needs assistance from outside.

If the principles of these measures and the form of the institutions to give effect to them can be settled in advance, in order that they may be in operation when the need arises, it is possible that taken together they may help the world to control the ebb and flow of the tides of economic activity which have, in the past, destroyed security of livelihood and endangered international peace.

All these matters will need to be handled in due course. The proposal that follows relates only to the mechanism of currency and exchange in international trading. It appears on the whole convenient to give it prior-

---

[72] Reproduced by permission of the Controller, Her Britannic Majesty's Stationery Office.

ity, because some general conclusions have to be reached under this head before much progress can be made with the other topics.

In preparing these proposals care has been taken to regard certain conditions, which the groundwork of an international economic system to be set up after the war should satisfy, if it is to prove durable:

(i) There should be the least possible interference with internal national policies, and the plan should not wander from the international *terrain*. Since such policies may have important repercussions on international relations, they cannot be left out of account. Nevertheless in the realm of internal policy the authority of the Governing Board of the proposed Institution should be limited to recommendations, or at the most to imposing conditions for the more extended enjoyment of the facilities which the Institution offers.

(ii) The technique of the plan must be capable of application, irrespective of the type and principle of government and economic policy existing in the prospective member States.

(iii) The management of the Institution must be genuinely international without preponderant power of veto or enforcement to any country or group; and the rights and privileges of the smaller countries must be safeguarded.

(iv) Some qualification of the right to act at pleasure is required by any agreement or treaty between nations. But in order that such arrangements may be fully voluntary so long as they last and terminable when they have become irksome, provision must be made for voiding the obligation at due notice. If many member States were to take advantage of this, the plan would have broken down. But if they are free to escape from its provisions if necessary they may be the more willing to go on accepting them.

(v) The plan must operate not only to the general advantage but also to the individual advantage of each of the participants, and must not require a special economic or financial sacrifice from certain countries. No participant must be asked to do or offer anything which is not to his own true long-term interest.

It must be emphasised that it is not for the Clearing Union to assume the burden of long term lending which is the proper task of some other institution. It is also necessary for it to have means of restraining improvident borrowers. But the Clearing Union must also seek to discourage creditor countries from leaving unused large liquid balances which ought to be devoted to some positive purpose. For excessive credit balances necessarily create excessive debit balances for some other party. In recognising that the creditor as well as the debtor may be responsible for a want of balance, the proposed institution would be breaking new ground.

I. THE OBJECTS OF THE PLAN

About the primary objects of an improved system of International Currency there is, today, a wide measure of agreement:

(a) We need an instrument of international currency having general acceptability between nations, so that blocked balances and bilateral clearings are unnecessary; that is to say, an instrument of currency used by each nation in its transactions with other nations, operating through whatever national organ, such as a Treasury or a Central Bank, is most appropriate, private individuals, businesses and banks other than Central Banks, each continuing to use their own national currency as heretofore.

(b) We need an orderly and agreed method of determining the relative exchange values of national currency units, so that unilateral action and competitive exchange depreciations are prevented.

(c) We need a quantum of international currency, which is neither determined in an unpredictable and irrelevant manner as, for example, by the technical progress of the gold industry, nor subject to large variations depending on the gold reserve policies of individual countries; but is governed by the actual current requirements of world commerce, and is also capable of deliberate expansion and contraction to offset deflationary and inflationary tendencies in effective world demand.

(d) We need a system possessed of an internal stabilising mechanism, by which pressure is exercised on any country whose balance of payments with the rest of the world is departing from equilibrium in either direction, so as to prevent movements which must create for its neighbours an equal but opposite want of balance.

(e) We need an agreed plan for starting off every country after the war with a stock of reserves appropriate to its importance in world commerce, so that without due anxiety it can set its house in order during the transitional period to full peacetime conditions.

(f) We need a central institution, of a purely technical and non-political character, to aid and support other international institutions concerned with the planning and regulation of the world's economic life.

(g) More generally, we need a means of reassurance to a troubled world, by which any country whose own affairs are conducted with due prudence is relieved of anxiety for causes which are not of its own making, concerning its ability to meet its international liabilities; and which will, therefore, make unnecessary those methods of restriction and discrimination which countries have adopted hitherto, not on their merits, but as measures of self-protection from disruptive outside forces.

2. There is also a growing measure of agreement about the general character of any solution of the problem likely to be successful. The particular proposals set forth below lay no claim to originality. They are an attempt to reduce to practical shape certain general ideas belonging to the contemporary climate of economic opinion, which have been given publicity in recent months by writers of several different nationalities.

It is difficult to see how any plan can be successful which does not use these general ideas, which are born of the spirit of the age. The actual details put forward below are offered, with no dogmatic intention, as the basis of discussion for criticism and improvement. For we cannot make progress without embodying the general underlying idea in a frame of actual working, which will bring out the practical and political difficulties to be faced and met if the breath of life is to inform it.

3. In one respect this particular plan will be found to be more ambitious and yet, at the same time, perhaps more workable than some of the variant versions of the same basic idea, in that it is fully international, being based on one general agreement and not on a multiplicity of bilateral arrangements. Doubtless proposals might be made by which bilateral arrangements could be fitted together so as to obtain some of the advantages of a multilateral scheme. But there will be many difficulties attendant on such adjustments. It may be doubted whether a comprehensive scheme will ever in fact be worked out, unless it can come into existence through a single act of creation made possible by the unity of purpose and energy of hope for better things to come, springing from the victory of the United Nations, when they have attained it, over immediate evil. That these proposals are ambitious is claimed, therefore to be not a drawback but an advantage.

4. The proposal is to establish a Currency Union, here designated an *International Clearing Union*, based on international bank-money, called (let us say) *bancor*, fixed (but not unalterably) in terms of gold and accepted as the equivalent of gold by the British Commonwealth and the United States and all the other members of the Union for the purpose of settling international balances. The Central Banks of all member States (and also of non-members) would keep accounts with the International Clearing Union through which they would be entitled to settle their exchange balances with one another at their par value as defined in terms of bancor. Countries having a favourable balance of payments with the rest of the world as a whole would find themselves in possession of a credit account with the Clearing Union, and those having an unfavourable balance would have a debit account. Measures would be necessary (see below) to prevent the piling up of credit and debit balances without limit, and the system would have failed in the long run if it did not possess sufficient capacity for self-equilibrium to secure this.

5. The idea underlying such a Union is simple, namely, to generalise the essential principle of banking as it is exhibited within any closed system. This principle is the necessary equality of credits and debits. If no credits can be removed outside the clearing system, but only transferred within it, the Union can never be in any difficulty as regards the honouring of cheques drawn upon it. It can make what advances it wishes to any of its members with the assurance that the proceeds can only be transferred to the clearing account of another member. Its sole task is to see to it that its members keep the rules and that the advances made to each of them are prudent and advisable for the Union as a whole.

II. THE PROVISIONS OF THE PLAN

6. The provisions proposed (the particular proportions and other details suggested being tentative as a basis of discussion) are the following:

(1) All the United Nations will be invited to become original members of the International Clearing Union. Other States may be invited to join subsequently. If ex-enemy States are invited to join, special conditions may be applied to them.

(2) The Governing Board of the Clearing Union shall be appointed by the Governments of the several member States (as provided in (12) below); the daily business with the Union and the technical arrangements being carried out through their Central Banks or other appropriate authorities.

(3) The member States will agree between themselves the initial values of their own currencies in terms of bancor. A member State may not subsequently alter the value of its currency in terms of bancor without the permission of the Governing Board except under the conditions stated below; but during the first five years after the inception of the system the Governing Board shall give special consideration to appeals for an adjustment in the exchange value of a national currency unit on the ground of unforeseen circumstances.

(4) The value of bancor in terms of gold shall be fixed by the Governing Board. Member States shall not purchase or acquire gold, directly or indirectly, at a price in terms of their national currencies in excess of the parity which corresponds to the value of their currency in terms of bancor and to the value of bancor in terms of gold. Their sales and purchases of gold shall not be otherwise restricted.

(5) Each member State shall have assigned to it a quota, which shall determine the measure of its responsibility in the management of the Union and of its right to enjoy the credit facilities provided by the Union. The initial quotas might be fixed by reference to the sum of each country's exports and imports on the average of (say) the three pre-war years, and might be (say) 75 per cent. of this amount, a special assessment being substituted in cases (of which there might be several) where this formula would be, for any reason, inappropriate. Subsequently, after the elapse of the transitional period, the quotas should be revised annually in accordance with the running average of each country's actual volume of trade in the three preceding years, rising to a five-year average when figures for five post-war years are available. The determination of a country's quota primarily by reference to the value of its foreign trade seems to offer the criterion most relevant to a plan which is chiefly concerned with the regulation of the foreign exchanges and of a country's international trade balance.

It is, however, a matter for discussion whether the formula for fixing quotas should also take account of other factors.

(6) Member States shall agree to accept payment of currency balances, due to them from other members, by a transfer of bancor to their credit in the books of the Clearing Union. They shall be entitled, subject to the conditions set forth below, to make transfers of bancor to other members which have the effect of overdrawing their own accounts with the Union, provided that the maximum debit balances thus created do not exceed their quota. The Clearing

Union may, at its discretion, charge a small commission or transfer fee in respect of transactions in its books for the purpose of meeting its current expenses or any other outgoings approved by the Governing Board.

(7) A member State shall pay to the Reserve Fund of the Clearing Union a charge of 1 per cent. per annum on the amount of its average balance in bancor, whether it is a credit or a debit balance, in excess of a quarter of its quota; and a further charge of 1 per cent. on its average balance, whether credit or debit, in excess of a half of its quota. Thus, only a country which keeps as nearly as possible in a state of international balance on the average of the year will escape this contribution. These charges are not absolutely essential to the scheme. But if they are found acceptable, they would be valuable and important inducements towards keeping a level balance, and a significant indication that the system looks on excessive credit balances with as critical an eye as on excessive debit balances, each being, indeed, the inevitable concomitant of the other. Any member State in debit may, after consultation with the Governing Board, borrow bancor from the balances of any member State in credit on such terms as may be mutually agreed, by which means each would avoid these contributions. The Governing Board may, at its discretion, remit the charges on credit balances, and increase correspondingly those on debit balances, if in its opinion unduly expansionist conditions are impending in the world economy.

(8) (a) A member State may not increase its debit balance by more than a *quarter* of its quota within a year without the permission of the Governing Board. If its debit balance has exceeded a quarter of its quota on the average of at least two years, it shall be entitled to reduce the value of its currency in terms of bancor provided that the reduction shall not exceed 5 per cent. without the consent of the Governing Board; but it shall not be entitled to repeat this procedure unless the Board is satisfied that this procedure is appropriate.

(b) The Governing Board may require from a member State having a debit balance reaching a *half* of its quota the deposit of suitable collateral against its debit balance. Such collateral shall, at the discretion of the Governing Board, take the form of gold, foreign or domestic currency or Government bonds, within the capacity of the member State. As a condition of allowing a member State to increase its debit balance to a figure in excess of a half of its quota, the Governing Board may require all or any of the following measures:

(i) a stated reduction in the value of the member's currency, if it deems that to be the suitable remedy;

(ii) the control of outward capital transactions if not already in force; and

(iii) the outright surrender of a suitable proportion of any separate gold or other liquid reserve in reduction of its debit balance.

Furthermore, the Governing Board may recommend to the Government of the member State any internal measures affecting its domestic economy which may appear to be appropriate to restore the equilibrium of its international balance.

(c) If a member State's debit balance has exceeded *three-quarters* of its quota on the average of at least a year and is excessive in the opinion of the Governing Board in relation to the total debit balances outstanding on the books of the Clearing Union, or is increasing at an excessive rate, it may, in addition, be asked by the Governing Board to take measures to improve its position, and, in the event of its failing to reduce its debit balance accordingly within two years, the Governing Board may declare that it is in default and no longer entitled to draw against its account except with the permission of the Governing Board.

(d) Each member State, on joining the system, shall agree to pay to the Clearing Union any payments due from it to a country in default towards the discharge of the latter's debit balance and to accept this arrangement in the event of falling into default itself. A member State which resigns from the Clearing Union without making approved arrangements for the discharge of any debit balance shall also be treated as in default.

(9) A member State whose credit balance has exceeded a half of its quota on the average of at least a year shall discuss with the Governing Board (but shall retain the ultimate decision in its own hands) what measures would be appropriate to restore the equilibrium of its international balances, including

(a) Measures for the expansion of domestic credit and domestic demand.

(b) The appreciation of its local currency in terms of bancor, or, alternatively, the encouragement of an increase in money rates of earnings;

(c) The reduction of tariffs and other discouragements against imports.

(d) International development loans.

(10) A member State shall be entitled to obtain a credit balance in terms of bancor by paying in gold to the Clearing Union for the credit of its clearing account. But no one is entitled to demand gold from the Union against a balance of bancor, since such balance is available only for transfer to another clearing account. The Governing Board of the Union shall, however, have the discretion to distribute

any gold in the possession of the Union between the members possessing credit balances in excess of a specified proportion of their quotas, proportionately to such balances, in reduction of their amount in excess of that proportion.

(11) The monetary reserves of a member State, viz., the Central Bank or other bank or Treasury deposits in excess of a working balance, shall not be held in another country except with the approval of the monetary authorities of that country.

(12) The Governing Board shall be appointed by the Governments of the member States, those with the larger quotas being entitled to appoint a member individually, and those with smaller quotas appointing in convenient political or geographical groups, so that the members would not exceed (say) 12 or 15 in number. Each representative on the Governing Board shall have a vote in proportion to the quotas of the State (or States) appointing him, except that on a proposal to increase a particular quota, a representative's voting power shall be measured by the quotas of the member States appointing him, increased by their credit balance or decreased by their debit balance, averaged in each case over the past two years. Each member State, which is not individually represented on the Governing Board, shall be entitled to appoint a permanent delegate to the Union to maintain contact with the Board and to act as liaison for daily business and for the exchange of information with the Executive of the Union. Such delegate shall be entitled to be present at the Governing Board when any matter is under consideration which specially concerns the State he represents, and to take part in the discussion.

(13) The Governing Board shall be entitled to reduce the quotas of members, all in the same specified proportion, if it seems necessary to correct in this manner an excess of world purchasing power. In that event, the provisions of 6 (8) shall be held to apply to the quotas as so reduced, provided that no member shall be required to reduce his actual overdraft at the date of the change, or be entitled by reason of this reduction to alter the value of his currency under 6 (8) (a), except after the expiry of two years. If the Governing Board subsequently desires to correct a potential deficiency of world purchasing power, it shall be entitled to restore the general level of quotas towards the original level.

(14) The Governing Board shall be entitled to ask and receive from each member State any relevant statistical or other information,

including a full disclosure of gold, external credit and debit balances and other external assets and liabilities, both public and private. So far as circumstances permit, it will be desirable that the member States shall consult with the Governing Board on important matters of policy likely to affect substantially their bancor balances or their financial relations with other members.

(15) Executives offices of the Union shall be situated in London and New York, with the Governing Board meeting alternately in London and Washington.

(16) Members shall be entitled to withdraw from the Union on a year's notice, subject to their making satisfactory arrangements to discharge any debit balance. They would not, of course, be able to employ any credit balance except by making transfers from it, either before or after their withdrawal, to the Clearing Accounts of other Central Banks. Similarly, it should be within the power of the Governing Board to require the withdrawal of a member, subject to the same notice, if the latter is in breach of agreements relating to the Clearing Union.

(17) The Central Banks of non-member States would be allowed to keep credit clearing accounts with the Union; and, indeed, it would be advisable for them to do so for the conduct of their trade with member States. But they would have no right to overdrafts and no say in the management.

(18) The Governing Board shall make an annual Report and shall convene an annual Assembly at which every member State shall be entitled to be represented individually and to move proposals. The principles and governing rules of the Union shall be the subject of reconsideration after five years' experience, if a majority of the Assembly desire it.

III. WHAT LIABILITIES OUGHT THE PLAN TO PLACE ON CREDITOR COUNTRIES?

7. It is not contemplated that either the debit or the credit balance of an individual country ought to exceed a certain maximum – let us say, its quota. In the case of debit balances this maximum has been made a rigid one, and, indeed, counter-measures are called for long before the maximum is reached. In the case of credit balances no rigid maximum has been proposed. For the appropriate provision might be to require the eventual cancellation or compulsory investment of persistent bancor credit balances accumulating in excess of a member's quota; and, however desir-

able this may be in principle, it might be felt to impose on creditor countries a heavier burden than they can be asked to accept before having had experience of the benefit to them of the working of the plan as a whole. If, on the other hand, the limitation were to take the form of the creditor country not being required to accept bancor in excess of a prescribed figure, this might impair the general acceptability of bancor, whilst at the same time conferring no real benefit on the creditor country itself. For, if it chose to avail itself of the limitation, it must either restrict its exports or be driven back on some form of bilateral payments agreements outside the Clearing Union, thus substituting a less acceptable asset for bancor balances which are based on the collective credit of all the member States and are available for payments to any of them, or attempt the probably temporary expedient of refusing to trade except on a gold basis.

8. The absence of a rigid maximum to credit balances does not impose on any member State, as might be supposed at first sight, an unlimited liability outside its own control. The liability of an individual member is determined, not by the quotas of the other members, but by its own policy in controlling its favourable balance of payments. The existence of the Clearing Union does not deprive a member State of any of the facilities which it now possesses for receiving payment for its exports. In the absence of the Clearing Union a creditor country can employ the proceeds of its exports to buy goods or to buy investments, or to make temporary advances and to hold temporary overseas balances, or to buy gold in the market. All these facilities will remain at its disposal. The difference is that in the absence of the Clearing Union, more or less automatic factors come into play to restrict the volume of its exports after the above means of receiving payment for them have been exhausted. Certain countries become unable to buy and, in addition to this, there is an automatic tendency towards a general slump in international trade and, as a result, a reduction in the exports of the creditor country. Thus, the effect of the Clearing Union is to give the creditor country a choice between voluntarily curtailing its exports to the same extent that they would have been involuntarily curtailed in the absence of the Clearing Union, or, alternatively, of allowing its exports to continue and accumulating the excess receipts in the form of bancor balances for the time being. Unless the removal of a factor causing the involuntary reduction of exports is reckoned a disadvantage, a creditor country incurs no burden but is, on the contrary, relieved, by being offered the additional option of receiving payment for its exports through the accumulation of a bancor balance.

9. If, therefore, a member State asks what governs the maximum liability which it incurs by entering the system, the answer is that this lies

entirely within its own control. No more is asked of it than that it should hold in bancor such surplus of its favourable balance of payments as it does not itself choose to employ in any other way, and only for so long as it does not so choose.

IV. SOME ADVANTAGES OF THE PLAN

10. The plan aims at the substitution of an expansionist, in place of a contractionist, pressure on world trade.

11. It effects this by allowing to each member State overdraft facilities of a defined amount. Thus each country is allowed a certain margin of resources and a certain interval of time within which to effect a balance in its economic relations with the rest of the world. These facilities are made possible by the constitution of the system itself and do not involve particular indebtedness between one member State and another. A country is in credit or debit with the Clearing Union as a whole. This means that the overdraft facilities, whilst a relief to some, are not a real burden to others. For the accumulation of a credit balance with the Clearing Union would resemble the importation of gold in signifying that the country holding it is abstaining voluntarily from the immediate use of purchasing power. But it would not involve, as would the importation of gold, the withdrawal of this purchasing power from circulation or the exercise of a deflationary and contractionist pressure on the whole world, including in the end the creditor country itself. Under the proposed plan, therefore, no country suffers injury (but on the contrary) by the fact that the command over resources, which it does not itself choose to employ for the time being, is not withdrawn from use. The accumulation of bancor credit does not curtail in the least its capacity or inducement either to produce or to consume.

12. In short, the analogy with a national banking system is complete. No depositor in a local bank suffers because the balances, which he leaves idle, are employed to finance the business of someone else. Just as the development of national banking systems served to offset a deflationary pressure which would have prevented otherwise the development of modern industry, so by extending the same principle into the international field we may hope to offset the contractionist pressure which might otherwise overwhelm in social disorder and disappointment the good hopes of our modern world. The substitution of a credit mechanism in place of hoarding would have repeated in the international field the same miracle, already performed in the domestic field, of turning a stone into bread.

13. There might be other ways of effecting the same objects temporarily or in part. For example, the United States might redistribute her gold.

Or there might be a number of bilateral arrangements having the effect of providing international overdrafts, as, for example, an agreement by the Federal Reserve Board to accumulate, if necessary, a large sterling balance at the Bank of England, accompanied by a great number of similar bilateral arrangements, amounting to some hundreds altogether, between these and all the other banks in the world. The objection to particular arrangements of this kind, in addition to their greater complexity, is that they are likely to be influenced by extraneous, political reasons; that they put individual countries in a position of particular obligation towards others; and that the distribution of the assistance between different countries may not correspond to need and to the real requirements, which are extremely difficult to foresee.

14. It should be much easier, and surely more satisfactory for all of us, to enter into a general and collective responsibility, applying to all countries alike, that a country finding itself in a creditor position *against the rest of the world as a whole* should enter into an arrangement not to allow this credit balance to exercise a contractionist pressure against world economy and, by repercussion, against the economy of the creditor country itself. This would give everyone the great assistance of multilateral clearing, whereby (for example) Great Britain could offset favourable balances arising out of her exports to Europe against unfavourable balances due to the United States or South America or elsewhere. How, indeed, can any country hope to start up trade with Europe during the relief and reconstruction period on any other terms?

15. The facilities offered will be of particular importance in the transitional period after the war, as soon as the initial shortages of supply have been overcome. Many countries will find a difficulty in paying for their imports, and will need time and resources before they can establish a readjustment. The efforts of each of these debtor countries to preserve its own equilibrium, by forcing its exports and by cutting off all imports which are not strictly necessary, will aggravate the problems of all the others.

On the other hand, if each feels free from undue pressure, the volume of international exchange will be increased and everyone will find it easier to re-establish equilibrium without injury to the standard of life anywhere. The creditor countries will benefit, hardly less than the debtors, by being given an interval of time in which to adjust their economies, during which they can safely move at their own pace without the result of exercising deflationary pressure on the rest of the world, and, by repercussion, on themselves.

16. It must, however, be emphasised that the provision by which the members of the Clearing Union start with substantial overdraft facilities

in hand will be mainly useful, just as the possession of any kind of reserve is useful, to allow time and method for necessary adjustments and a comfortable safeguard behind which the unforeseen and the unexpected can be faced with equanimity. Obviously, it does not by itself provide any long-term solution against a continuing disequilibrium, for in due course the more improvident and the more impecunious, left to themselves, would have run through their resources. But, if the purpose of the overdraft facilities is mainly to give time for adjustments, we have to make sure, so far as possible, that they will be made. We must have, therefore, some rules and some machinery to secure that equilibrium is restored. A tentative attempt to provide for this has been made above. Perhaps it might be strengthened and improved.

17. The provisions suggested differ in one important respect from the pre-war system because they aim at putting some part of the responsibility for adjustment on the creditor country as well as on the debtor. This is an attempt to recover one of the advantages which were enjoyed in the 19th century, when a flow of gold due to a favourable balance in favour of London and Paris, which were then the main creditor centres, immediately produced an expansionist pressure and increased foreign lending in those markets, but which has been lost since New York succeeded to the position of main creditor, as a result of gold movements failing in their effect, of the breakdown of international borrowing and of the frequent flight of loose funds from one depository to another. The object is that the creditor should not be allowed to remain entirely passive. For if he is, an intolerably heavy task may be laid on the debtor country, which is already for that very reason in the weaker position.

18. If, indeed, a country lacks the productive capacity to maintain its standard of life, then a reduction in this standard is not avoidable. If its wage and price levels in terms of money are out of line with those elsewhere, a change in the rate of its foreign exchange is inevitable. But if, possessing the productive capacity, it lacks markets because of restrictive policies throughout the world, then the remedy lies in expanding its opportunities for export by removal of the restrictive pressure. We are too ready to-day to assume the inevitability of unbalanced trade positions, thus making the opposite error to those who assumed the tendency of exports and imports to equality. It used to be supposed, without sufficient reason, that effective demand is always properly adjusted throughout the world; we now tend to assume, equally without sufficient reason, that it never can be. On the contrary, there is great force in the contention that, if active employment and ample purchasing power can be sustained in the main centres of the world trade, the problem of surpluses and unwanted

exports will largely disappear, even though, under the most prosperous conditions, there may remain some disturbances of trade and unforeseen situations requiring special remedies.

V. THE DAILY MANAGEMENT OF THE EXCHANGES UNDER THE PLAN

19. The Clearing Union restores unfettered multilateral clearing between its members. Compare this with the difficulties and complications of a large number of bilateral agreements. Compare, above all, the provisions by which a country, taking improper advantage of a payments agreement (for the system is, in fact, a generalised payments agreement), as Germany did before the war, is dealt with not by a single country (which may not be strong enough to act effectively in isolation or cannot afford to incur the diplomatic odium of isolated action), but by the system as a whole. If the argument is used that the Clearing Union may have difficulty in disciplining a misbehaving country and in avoiding consequential loss, with what much greater force can we urge this objection against a multiplicity of separate bilateral payments agreements.

20. Thus we should not only obtain the advantages, without the disadvantages, of an international gold currency, but we might enjoy these advantages more widely than was ever possible in practice with the old system under which at any given time only a minority of countries were actually working with free exchanges. In conditions of multilateral clearing, exchange dealings would be carried on as freely as in the best days of the gold standard, without its being necessary to ask anyone to accept special or onerous conditions.

21. The principles governing transactions are: first, that the Clearing Union is set up, not for the transaction of daily business between individual traders or banks, but for the clearing and settlement of the ultimate outstanding balances between Central Banks (and certain other supernational Institutions), such as would have been settled under the old gold standard by the shipment or the earmarking of gold, and should not trespass unnecessarily beyond this field; and, second, that its purpose is to increase *freedom* in international commerce and not to multiply interferences or compulsions.

22. Many Central Banks have found great advantage in centralising with themselves or with an Exchange Control the supply and demand of all foreign exchange, thus dispensing with an outside exchange market, though continuing to accommodate individuals through the existing banks and not directly. The further extension of such arrangements would

be consonant with the general purposes of the Clearing Union, inasmuch as they would promote order and discipline in international exchange transactions in detail as well as in general. The same is true of the control of Capital Movements, further described below, which many States are likely to wish to impose on their own nationals. But the structure of the proposed Clearing Union does not require such measures of centralisation or of control on the part of a member State. It is, for example, consistent alike with the type of Exchange Control now established in the United Kingdom or with the system now operating in the United States. The Union does not prevent private holdings of foreign currency or private dealings in exchange or international capital movements, if these have been approved or allowed by the member States concerned. Central Banks can deal direct with one another as heretofore. No transaction in bancor will take place except when a member State or its Central Bank is exercising the right to pay in it. In no case is there any direct control of capital movements by the Union, even in the case of 6 (8) (b) (ii) above, but only by the member States themselves through their own institutions. Thus the fabric of international banking organisation, built up by long experience to satisfy practical needs, would be left as undisturbed as possible.

23. It is not necessary to interfere with the discretion of countries which desire to maintain a special intimacy within a particular group of countries associated by geographical or political ties, such as the existing sterling area, or groups, like the Latin Union of former days, which may come into existence covering, for example, the countries of North America or those of South America, or the groups now under active discussion, including Poland and Czechoslovakia or certain of the Balkan States. There is no reason why such countries should not be allowed a double position, both as members of the Clearing Union in their own right with their proper quota, and also as making use of another financial centre along traditional lines, as, for example, Australia and India with London, or certain American countries with New York. In this case, their accounts with the Clearing Union would be in exactly the same position as the independent gold reserves which they now maintain, and they would have no occasion to modify in any way their present practices in the conduct of daily business.

24. There might be other cases, however, in which a dependency or a member of a federal union would merge its currency identity in that of a mother country, with a quota appropriately adjusted to the merged currency area as a whole, and not enjoy a separate individual membership of the Clearing Union, as, for example, the States of a Federal Union, the French colonies or the British Crown Colonies.

25. At the same time countries, which do not belong to a special geographical or political group, would be expected to keep their reserve balances with the Clearing Union and not with one another. It has, therefore, been laid down that balances may not be held in another country except with the approval of the monetary authorities of that country; and, in order that sterling and dollars might not appear to compete with bancor for the purpose of reserve balances, the United Kingdom and the United States might agree together that they would not accept the reserve balances of other countries in excess of normal working balances – except in the case of banks definitely belonging to a Sterling Area or Dollar Area group.

VI. THE POSITION OF GOLD UNDER THE PLAN

26. Gold still possesses great psychological value which is not being diminished by current events; and the desire to possess a gold reserve against unforeseen contingencies is likely to remain. Gold also has the merit of providing in point of form (whatever the underlying realities may be) an uncontroversial standard of value for international purposes, for which it would not yet be easy to find a serviceable substitute. Moreover, by supplying an automatic means for settling some part of the favourable balances of the creditor countries, the current gold production of the world and the remnant of of gold reserves held outside the United States may still have a useful part to play. Nor is it reasonable to ask the United States to de-monetise the stock of gold which is the basis of its impregnable liquidity. What, in the long run, the world may decide to do with gold is another matter. The purpose of the Clearing Union is to supplant gold as a governing factor, but not to dispense with it.

27. The international bank-money which we have designated bancor is defined in terms of a weight of gold. Since the national currencies of the member States are given a defined exchange value in terms of bancor, it follows that they would each have a defined gold content which would be their official buying price for gold, above which they must not pay. The fact that a member State is entitled to obtain a credit in terms of bancor by paying actual gold to the credit of its clearing account, secures a steady and ascertained purchaser for the output of the gold-producing countries, and for countries holding a large reserve of gold. Thus the position of producers and holders of gold is not affected adversely, and is, indeed, improved.

28. Central Banks would be entitled to retain their separate gold reserves and ship gold to one another, provided they did not pay a price above parity; they could coin gold and put it into circulation, and, generally speaking, do what they liked with it.

29. One limitation only would be, for obvious reasons, essential. No member State would be entitled to demand gold from the Clearing Union against its balance of bancor; for bancor is available only for transfer to another clearing account. Thus between gold and bancor itself there would be a one-way convertibility, such as ruled frequently before the war with national currencies which were on what was called a "gold exchange standard." This need not mean that the Clearing Union would only receive gold and never pay it out. It has been provided above that, if the Clearing Union finds itself in possession of a stock of gold, the Governing Board shall have discretion to distribute the surplus between those possessing credit balances in bancor, proportionately to such balances in reduction of their amount.

30. The question has been raised whether these arrangements are compatible with the retention by individual member States of a full gold standard with two-way convertibility, so that, for example, any foreign central bank acquiring dollars could use them to obtain gold for export. It is not evident that a good purpose would be served by this. But it need not be prohibited, and if any member State should prefer to maintain full convertibility for internal purposes it could protect itself from any abuse of the system or inconvenient consequences by providing that gold could only be exported under licence.

31. The value of bancor in terms of gold is fixed but not unalterably. The power to vary its value might have to be exercised if the stocks of gold tendered to the Union were to be excessive. No object would be served by attempting further to peer into the future or to prophesy the ultimate outcome.

VII. THE CONTROL OF CAPITAL MOVEMENTS

32. There is no country which can, in future, safely allow the flight of funds for political reasons or to evade domestic taxation or in anticipation of the owner turning refugee. Equally, there is no country that can safely receive fugitive funds, which constitute an unwanted import of capital, yet cannot safely be used for fixed investment.

33. For these reasons it is widely held that control of capital movements, both inward and outward, should be a permanent feature of the post-war system. It is an objection to this that control, if it is to be effective, probably requires the machinery of exchange control for all transactions, even though a general permission is given to all remittances in respect of current trade. Thus those countries which have for the time being no reason to fear, and may indeed welcome, outward capital move-

ments, may be reluctant to impose this machinery, even though a general permission for capital, as well as current, transactions reduces it to being no more than a machinery of record. On the other hand, such control will be more difficult to work by unilateral action on the part of those countries which cannot afford to dispense with it, especially in the absence of a postal censorship, if movements of capital cannot be controlled at both ends. It would, therefore, be of great advantage if the United States, as well as other members of the Clearing Union, would adopt machinery similar to that which the British Exchange Control has now gone a long way towards perfecting. Nevertheless, the universal establishment of a control of capital movements cannot be regarded as essential to the operation of the Clearing Union; and the method and degree of such control should therefore be left to the decision of each member State. Some less drastic way might be found by which countries, not themselves controlling outward capital movements, can deter inward movements not approved by the countries from which they originate.

34. The position of abnormal balances in overseas ownership held in various countries at the end of the war presents a problem of considerable importance and special difficulty. A country in which a large volume of such balances is held could not, unless it is in a creditor position, afford the risk of having to redeem them in bancor on a substantial scale, if this would have the effect of depleting its bancor resources at the outset. At the same time, it is very desirable that the countries owning these balances should be able to regard them as liquid, at any rate over and above the amounts which they can afford to lock up under an agreed programme of funding or long-term expenditure. Perhaps there should be some special over-riding provision for dealing with the transitional period only by which, through the aid of the Clearing Union, such balances would remain liquid and convertible into bancor by the creditor country whilst there would be no corresponding strain on the bancor resources of the debtor country, or, at any rate, the resulting strain would be spread over a period.

35. The advocacy of a control of capital movements must not be taken to mean that the era of international investment should be brought to an end. On the contrary, the system contemplated should greatly facilitate the restoration of international loans and credits for legitimate purposes. The object, and it is a vital object, is to have a means

(a) of distinguishing long-term loans by creditor countries, which help to maintain equilibrium and develop the world's resources, from movements of funds out of debtor countries which lack the means to finance them; and

(b) of controlling short-term speculative movements or flights of currency whether out of debtor countries or from one creditor country to another.

36. It should be emphasised that the purpose of the overdrafts of bancor permitted by the Clearing Union is, not to facilitate long-term, or even medium-term, credits to be made by debtor countries which cannot afford them, but to allow time and a breathing space for adjustments and for averaging one period with another to all member States alike, whether in the long run they are well-placed to develop a forward international loan policy or whether their prospects of profitable new development in excess of their own resources justifies them in long-term borrowing. The machinery and organisation of international medium-term and long-term lending is another aspect of post-war economic policy, not less important than the purposes which the Clearing Union seeks to serve, but requiring another, complementary institution.

VIII. RELATION OF THE CLEARING UNION
TO COMMERCIAL POLICY

37. The special protective expedients which were developed between the two wars were sometimes due to political, social or industrial reasons. But frequently they were nothing more than forced and undesired dodges to protect an unbalanced position of a country's overseas payments. The new system, by helping to provide a register of the size and whereabouts of the aggregate debtor and creditor positions respectively, and an indication whether it is reasonable for a particular country to adopt special expedients as a temporary measure to assist in regaining equilibrium in its balance of payments, would make it possible to establish a general rule not to adopt them, subject to the indicated exceptions.

38. The existence of the Clearing Union would make it possible for member States contracting commercial agreements to use their respective debit and credit positions with the Clearing Union as a test, though this test by itself would not be complete. Thus, the contracting parties, whilst agreeing to clauses in a commercial agreement forbidding, in general, the use of certain measures or expedients in their mutual trade relations, might make this agreement subject to special relaxations if the state of their respective clearing accounts satisfied an agreed criterion. For example, an agreement might provide that, in the event of one of the contracting States having a debit balance with the Clearing Union exceeding a specified proportion of its quota on the average of a period it should be free to resort to import regulation or to barter trade agreements or to higher import

duties of a type which was restricted under the agreement in normal circumstances. Protected by the possibility of such temporary indulgences, the members of the Clearing Union should feel much more confidence in moving towards the withdrawal of other and more dislocating forms of protection and discrimination and in accepting the prohibition of the worst of them from the outset. In any case, it should be laid down that members of the Union would not allow or suffer among themselves any restrictions on the disposal of receipts arising out of current trade or "invisible" income.

IX. THE USE OF THE CLEARING UNION FOR OTHER INTERNATIONAL PURPOSES

39. The Clearing Union might become the instrument and the support of international policies in addition to those which it is its primary purpose to promote. This deserves the greatest possible emphasis. The Union might become the pivot of the future economic government of the world. Without it, other more desirable developments will find themselves impeded and unsupported. With it, they will fall into their place as parts of an ordered scheme. No one of the following suggestions is a necessary part of the plan. But they are illustrations of the additional purposes of high importance and value which the Union, once established, might be able to serve:

(1) The Union might set up a clearing account in favour of international bodies charged with post-war relief, rehabilitation and reconstruction. But it could go much further than this. For it might supplement contributions received from other sources by granting preliminary overdraft facilities in favour of these bodies, the overdraft being discharged over a period of years out of the Reserve Fund of the Union, or, if necessary, out of a levy on surplus credit balances. So far as this method is adopted it would be possible to avoid asking any country to assume a burdensome commitment for relief and reconstruction, since the resources would be provided in the first instance by those countries having credit clearing accounts for which they have no immediate use and are voluntarily leaving idle, and in the long run by those countries which have a chronic international surplus for which they have no beneficial employment.

(2) The Union might set up an account in favour of any super-national policing body which may be charged with the duty of preserving the peace and maintaining international order. If any country were

to infringe its properly authorised orders, the policing body might be entitled to request the Governors of the Clearing Union to hold the clearing account of the delinquent country to its order and permit no further transactions on the account except by its authority. This would provide an excellent machinery for enforcing a financial blockade.

(3) The Union might set up an account in favour of international bodies charged with the management of a Commodity Control, and might finance stocks of commodities held by such bodies, allowing them overdraft facilities on their accounts up to an agreed maximum. By this means the financial problem of buffer stocks and "evernormal granaries" could be effectively attacked.

(4) The Union might be linked up with a Board for International Investment. It might act on behalf of such a Board and collect for them the annual service of their loans by automatically debiting the clearing account of the country concerned. The statistics of the clearing accounts of the member-States would give a reliable indication as to which countries were in a position to finance the Investment Board, with the advantage of shifting the whole system of clearing credits and debits nearer to equilibrium.

(5) There are various methods by which the Clearing Union could use its influence and its powers to maintain stability of prices and to control the Trade Cycle. If an International Economic Board is established, this Board and the Clearing Union might be expected to work in close collaboration to their mutual advantage. If an International Investment or Development Corporation is also set up together with a scheme of Commodity Controls for the control of stocks of the staple primary products, we might come to possess in these three Institutions a powerful means of combating the evils of the Trade Cycle, by exercising contractionist or expansionist influence on the system as a whole or on particular sections. This is a large and important question which cannot be discussed adequately in this paper; and need not be examined at length in this place because it does not raise any important issues affecting the fundamental constitution of the proposed Union. It is mentioned here to complete the picture of the wider purposes which the foundation of the Clearing Union might be made to serve.

40. The facility of applying the Clearing Union plan to these several purposes arises out of a fundamental characteristic which is worth

pointing out, since it distinguishes the plan from those proposals which try to develop the same basic principle along bilateral lines and is one of the grounds on which the Plan can claim superior merit. This might be described as its "anonymous" or "impersonal" quality. No particular member States have to engage their own resources as such to the support of other particular States or of any of the international projects or policies adopted. They have only to agree in general that, if they find themselves with surplus resources which for the time being they do not themselves wish to employ, these resources may go into the general pool and be put to work on approved purposes. This costs the surplus country nothing because it is not asked to part permanently, or even for any specified period, with such resources, which it remains free to expend and employ for its own purposes whenever it chooses; in which case the burden of finance is passed on to the next recipient, again for only so long as the recipient has no use for the money. As pointed out above, this merely amounts to extending to the international sphere the methods of any domestic banking system, which are in the same sense "impersonal" inasmuch as there is no call on the particular depositor either to support as such the purposes for which his banker makes advances or to forgo permanently the use of his deposit. There is no countervailing objection except that which applies equally to the technique of domestic banking, namely that it is capable of the abuse of creating excessive purchasing power and hence an inflation of prices. In our efforts to avoid the opposite evil, we must not lose sight of this risk, to which there is an allusion in 39 (5) above. But it is no more reason for refusing the advantages of international banking than the similar risk in the domestic field is a reason to return to the practices of the 17th century goldsmiths (which are what we are still following in the international field) and to forgo the vast expansion of production which banking principles have made possible. Where financial contributions are required for some purpose of general advantage, it is a great facility not to have to ask for specific contributions from any named country, but to depend rather on the anonymous and impersonal aid of the system as a whole. We have here a genuine organ of truly international government.

X. THE TRANSITIONAL ARRANGEMENTS

41. It would be of great advantage to agree the general principles of the Clearing Union before the end of the war, with a view to bringing it into operation at an early date after the termination of hostilities. Major plans will be more easily brought to birth in the first energy of victory and whilst the active spirit of united action still persists, than in the days of exhaustion and reaction from so much effort which may well follow a

little later. Such a proposal presents, however, something of a dilemma. On the one hand, many countries will be in particular need of reserves of overseas resources in the period immediately after the war. On the other hand, goods will be in short supply and the prevention of inflationary international conditions of much more importance for the time being than the opposite. The expansionist tendency of the plan, which is a leading recommendation of it as soon as peace-time output is restored and the productive capacity of the world is in running order, might be a danger in the early days of a sellers' market and an excess of demand over supply.

42. A reconciliation of these divergent purposes is not easily found until we know more than is known at present about the means to be adopted to finance post-war relief and reconstruction. If the intention is to provide resources on liberal and comprehensive lines outside the resources made available by the Clearing Union and additional to them, it might be better for such specific aid to take the place of the proposed overdrafts during the "relief" period of (say) two years. In this case credit clearing balances would be limited to the amount of gold delivered to the Union, and the overdraft facilities created by the Union in favour of the Relief Council, the International Investment Board or the Commodity Controls. Nevertheless, the immediate establishment of the Clearing Union would not be incompatible with provisional arrangements, which could take alternative forms according to the character of the other "relief" arrangements, qualifying and limiting the overdraft quotas. Overdraft quotas might be allowed on a reduced scale during the transitional period. Or it might be proper to provide that countries in receipt of relief or Lend-Lease assistance should not have access at the same time to overdraft facilities, and that the latter should only become available when the former had come to an end. If, on the other hand, relief from outside sources looks like being inadequate from the outset, the overdraft quotas may be even more necessary at the outset than later on.

43. We must not be over-cautious. A rapid economic restoration may lighten the tasks of the diplomatists and the politicians in the resettlement of the world and the restoration of social order. For Great Britain and other countries outside the "relief" areas the possibility of exports sufficient to sustain their standard of life is bound up with good and expanding markets. We cannot afford to wait too long for this, and we must not allow excessive caution to condemn us to perdition. Unless the Union is a going concern, the problem of proper "timing" will be nearly insoluble. It is sufficient at this stage to point out that the problem of timing must not be overlooked, but that the Union is capable of being used so as to aid rather than impede its solution.

XI. CONCLUSION

44. It has been suggested that so ambitious a proposal is open to criticism on the ground that it requires from the members of the Union a greater surrender of their sovereign rights than they will readily concede. But no greater surrender is required than in a commercial treaty. The obligations will be entered into voluntarily and can be terminated on certain conditions by giving notice.

45. A greater readiness to accept super-national arrangements must be required in the post-war world. If the arrangements proposed can be described as a measure of financial disarmament, there is nothing here which we need be reluctant to accept ourselves or to ask of others. It is an advantage, and not a disadvantage, of the scheme that it invites the member States to abandon that licence to promote indiscipline, disorder and bad-neighbourliness which, to the general disadvantage, they have been free to exercise hitherto.

46. The plan makes a beginning at the future economic ordering of the world between nations and "the winning of the peace." It might help to create the conditions and the atmosphere in which much else would be made easier.

B. Using the SDR as a Lever to Reform the International Monetary System*

REPORT OF AN SDR WORKING PARTY

May 2014

Foreword

In 2009 the *Triffin International Foundation* launched, under the chairmanship of Alexandre Lamfalussy and with the support of the *Compagnia di San Paolo di Torino*, the "Triffin 21 Initiative": this was aimed at addressing "the fundamental role" in the recent crisis "played by a flaw in the present monetary arrangements" which Robert Triffin had clearly identified and denounced in his time. The Triffin International Foundation argued "as long as this flaw is not addressed, one cannot expect to achieve lasting financial stability and sustainable economic growth".

This initiative first gave rise to the inaugural lecture "The Ghost of Bancor: the Economic Crisis and Global Monetary Disorder" given in Louvain-la-Neuve on 25 February 2010 by the late Tommaso Padoa-Schioppa[73], and to the symposium "Towards a World Reserve Currency" organized in Turin in May 2010 by the Compagnia di San Paolo and Triffin International Foundation[74].

Moreover, in October 2010, Michel Camdessus, Alexandre Lamfalussy, and Tommaso Padoa-Schioppa, convened, with the moral support of the Triffin International Foundation, a group of 18 former Ministers, Governors, Heads of International Institutions and Senior officials, which took the name of *Palais Royal Initiative* (PRI), to evaluate the international monetary system (IMS) and to propose changes that might be needed to stabilize it and reduce the likelihood of future failures. On February 2011, the PRI delivered to the Chairman of the G-20 the report "Reform of the International Monetary System: a Cooperative Approach for the Twenty First Century", which was communicated to the governments of the member countries, in preparation of the G-20 Summit that was held in Cannes in November 2011[75].

---

* Also available as the *The Federalist Debate Papers* No. 1- Supplement to *The Federalist Debate* No. 2, July 2014, Year XXVII.

[73] http://www.uclouvain.be/cps/ucl/doc/triffin/documents/TPS_EN_finale_clean.pdf.

[74] http://www.federalist-debate.org/index.php/component/k2/item/40-an-international-colloquium-on-the-initiative-triffin-21.

[75] The report, along with introductory documents and working papers, can be found in Jack T. Boorman and André Icard (eds.), *Reform of the International Monetary System. The Palais Royal Initiative*, New Delhi, 2011.

The Palais-Royal report made 18 concrete suggestions in the domains of Economic and Financial policies, Exchange rates, Global Liquidity, SDRs, and Governance. Taking on board a number of these suggestions, the G-20 Presidency proposed to the Cannes Summit five areas for reform: surveillance of the global economy and financial system, global financial safety nets, management of global capital flows, reserve assets and reserve currencies, and IMS governance. However, at the Summit, these proposals were crowded out by the onset of the sovereign debt crisis, and relatively little ground was covered on the reform of the IMS. The bulk of the PRI suggestions and of the G-20 proposals largely inspired by them are still available for consideration by public authorities.

Nevertheless, the PRI report, in its section V, remained relatively succinct regarding the role of the SDR and indicated in a footnote: "Suggestions 13 to 15 (devoted to SDRs) have not been fully developed but there was a near consensus amongst the group on proposing that the subject merits serious discussions". This is the research area of this working party[76], which was initiated by the Triffin International Foundation, in the aftermath of the conference organized in Brussels on 3-4 October 2011 on "The International Monetary System: Sustainability and Reform Proposals", to celebrate the 100th anniversary of Robert Triffin.[77]

The SDR Working Party's Report

The present report starts (section I) by reaffirming the existence of a "built-in-destabilizer" in the present IMS, which is based on the use of national currencies – mainly the US dollar – as reserve currencies, and by presenting the theoretical first-best solution, which unfortunately is likely to remain out of reach for long. Nevertheless, the need to break free from the status quo leads to re-explore the potential role of the SDR (section II) for strengthening monetary and financial stability, in the present globalized and multi-polar world. Then, based on analytic elements, the report makes nine suggestions (A to I) aimed at overcoming the present deficiencies in the functioning of the IMS through an enhancement of official SDRs (section III) and the development of a private SDR market (section IV).

---

[76] The composition of the Working Party is detailed in annex 1. Financial support was kindly provided by the *Centre for Studies on Federalism* and *CNH Industrial.*

[77] The proceedings of this conference were edited by Jean-Claude Koeune and Alexandre Lamfalussy under the title *À la recherche d'un nouvel ordre monétaire mondial – In Search of a New World Monetary Order*, Brussels, 2012.

I. The systemic flaw in the present IMS and the basic principles for a first best solution

1. Understanding the "built-in destabilizer" in the present IMS.

The goal and functions of an efficient IMS are essentially to provide for two intertwined global public goods: supplying adequate global liquidity to ensure global economic growth in balanced monetary conditions; and minimizing the costs to activity and employment when global external disequilibria need to adjust.

The systemic defect of the present arrangements on which we focus is due to the failure to resolve the Triffin dilemma. This consists in the difficult choice, for the country or the monetary area issuing the reserve currency, between going ever deeper into debt in order to satisfy the growing world demand for liquidity, with the danger that this will undermine its creditworthiness on the one hand, or failing to satisfy this demand by giving priority to preserving its creditworthiness on the other hand. This basic fact is independent of the exchange-rate regime, whether a general peg like the past Bretton Woods system or all kinds of "clean" or "dirty" floating regimes, since by definition, with such an arrangement, the reserve currency is a liability of the issuer toward the other reserve-holding users, who invest it into liquid financial papers issued by the key-currency country (Treasury bills and bank CDs). Indeed, by virtue of the inner nature of a key-currency, its foreign official holders do not simply deposit its amounts on their accounts with the issuing Central Bank but re-inject them into financial assets issued by the reserve currency economy (automatic capital inflows). Therefore, whatever the exchange-rate regime, the liquidity effect created abroad by the variation in the holdings of external reserves in this key-currency is not offset by a contrary variation in the monetary base of the issuer. Thus any national currency used as foreign reserve by other countries provokes a significant spillover on global liquidity conditions.

Actually, since the creation of the Bretton Woods system and even after its breakdown, this kind of spillover has prevailed, most often in an expansionary fashion, and has given rise to global monetary waves. In the last decade, this phenomenon has been amplified by an unprecedented accumulation of reserves based on large and often persisting current and capital account imbalances, in a world of rapidly growing global trade and fast development of international financial markets prone to frequent episodes of instability.

As the international use of a national currency automatically relaxes the external constraint on the issuer country and allows it to follow, too easily, macroeconomic policies that prioritize domestic full employment, even if there are negative spillovers on the rest of the world, one cannot exclude the possibility that such growing global imbalances lead to massive reserve accumulation and increasing financial instability as explained by the Triffin dilemma.

Indeed, Triffin foresaw, in the last published version[78] of his analysis of the asymmetries generated by the dollar-system, the development of a vicious circle of disequilibria he named a "built-in destabilizer", which affects both the reserve currency country and the other economies, and relies upon two intertwined mechanical channels: first the weakening of the external constraint on the issuer of the reserve currency, which tends to exacerbate its macroeconomic imbalances by pushing down its saving rate and, second, the transmission to the rest of the world of the monetary conditions prevailing in the reserve currency country. Other creditor central banks, concerned by a growing instability risk and sometimes also motivated by mercantilist objectives, are inclined to pile up additional reserves, resist appreciation of their currencies, and re-inject in reserve currency assets their excess holdings, lowering these assets' yields, especially at the long end of the curve.

As a result, global liquidity conditions cannot be adequately regulated, reinforcing the cyclicality of global economic trends, and braking the macroeconomic and structural adjustments in both deficit and surplus countries. Whatever the initial causes of the macroeconomic imbalances, the present international monetary system allows them to persist unduly.

This mechanism, theorized by Triffin in 1991, well illustrates the process that developed twenty years later in an environment of rapidly growing global trade and international capital flows, which ended up in the 2007-2008 crises and their aftermath. Indeed, one can observe the parallel trend between accommodative monetary policies in the United States with ever growing over-consumption and indebtedness, and their mirror image in the form of growing current account surpluses for the rest of the world. This fact, possibly compounded by domestic policy distortions such as mercantilist behavior which may encourage excess savings outside the USA, helps explain why an excess demand for new external reserves is fed primarily by concerns over financial instability.

---

[78]   Triffin, Robert, "The IMS (International Monetary System...or Scandal?) and the EMS (European Monetary System...or Success?)", Jean Monnet lecture, European University Institute, Florence, *Banca Nazionale del Lavoro Quarterly Review*, No. 179, December 1991.

In turn this excess demand for reserves automatically tends to nourish the US deficit, worsening the global disequilibrium and the financial exposure of the banking system and calling for further monetary and fiscal stimuli in the US economy. Therefore, Triffin's "built-in destabilizer" hypothesis, confirmed to a large extent by the events of the last decade, could explain why an IMS based on reserve currencies is largely responsible for a "global vicious circle" which generates global monetary waves and systemic instability with boom-and-bust episodes, and results in a loss of welfare for all countries, including those issuing reserve currencies.

Irrespective of the position economists have taken on this explanatory hypothesis, global disequilibria registered in the last decade have shown a rising trend. Since the use of the dollar as the main reserve currency produces significant policy spillovers and external liquidity effects, there is a clear case for examining the way to internalize them in either a systemic/centralized fashion, or at the least in a cooperative one. At the national level, economists long ago agreed on the need to control the spillovers generated by the banking system's money creation through a "Central Bank" charged with regulating bank liquidity by issuing or destroying its own liabilities used as the national currency. At the global level, this very same need should logically lead to the creation of a single global reserve currency issued by a single multilateral central bank, which could regulate the global liquidity needed for a globalized economy in a rational way. Nation-based monetary policies, by showing their inability to regulate properly global liquidity and financial markets, have revealed the need for collective action.

2. The long-term need for a systemic reform eliminating the Triffin dilemma.

The best solution would be to create a multilateral reserve currency, issued by an IMF transformed into a global central bank, in other words a liquid liability that is not the debt of any individual country. The purpose is to make feasible a symmetric regulation of global liquidities able to contribute to offset deflationary or inflationary tendencies in effective world demand. External constraint is inherently asymmetric and deflationary as it tends to depress world demand because the constraint upon deficit countries to balance their account is stronger than the disposition of surplus economies to adjust by saving less. Indeed, as initially proposed by Keynes at Bretton Woods in 1944 and taken up repeatedly by Triffin since the 1950s, only a globally created reserve currency – i.e. a liquid liability of the IMF (or another IFI with near-universal membership) – can make up for the contractionary bias of external adjustment while satisfying world demand for reserves without creating any national debt, because by definition there is no net foreign liability for the world as a whole, as an increase in the IMF's liabilities does not increase the deficit of any country.

We take it that the world has decided to stay with a floating exchange-rate system. We also believe it to be desirable that the international reserve currency becomes multilateral, with its issuer (the IMF) getting the means to actively regulate issues of reserve assets in both directions. This requires not only making the IMF a genuine lender-of-last-resort (LOLR), but also transforming it into a global monetary authority capable of preventing the creation of global excess reserves as much as the occurrence of a global shortage of reserves. Of course, each national monetary authority would remain free to set different objectives for its own economy and to diverge from the global stability policy; that is inherent in floating.

However, one must admit that the first-best solution of global liquidity conditions being determined by a world central bank is out of reach in today's world because political forces, voting, decision-making processes and regulations remain mostly national while economic and financial developments are global. This divergence allows national and vested interests to neglect global public good considerations and to override world welfare concerns. One must therefore search for a second-best solution that is compatible with existing constraints and which could ultimately evolve toward the first-best solution.

II. Making the best out of the current system: the SDR as a key element for an improved IMS

3. The medium-term need for a pragmatic step towards a systemic solution.

The Working Party is aware that in the current circumstances getting agreement on necessary adjustments would be the most valuable reform, but in the absence of significant progress in this field, it focused on a specific solution involving the use of the SDR.

Searching for a second best solution raises the question: is there a pragmatic way to make the best out of the current system and to correct the main deficiencies in the current management of the IMS, using existing instruments? By good fortune such an instrument already exists in the form of the Special Drawing Right (SDR), which "was originally conceived in the 1960s as an official reserve asset that would be both supplement to and substitute for the US dollar"[79]. Indeed, the Committee of Twenty that met from 1972 to 1974 visualized this asset becoming the basic asset of the international monetary system. However this vision has not been realized because nations pursued their individual short-run self-interest, which resulted in a continuation of the reserve currency system. Even though it has so far fallen short of expectations, clearly the SDR should be a good candidate for playing a catalytic role in a pragmatic and progressive approach.

The present excessive accumulation of reserves has its main proximate cause in global macroeconomic instability along with mercantilist behavior and the induced central banks' desire to be able to conduct autonomous intervention policies free from the constraints of IMF conditionality. It is permitted by large and persisting current account surpluses or, in some cases, large borrowings on unstable international financial markets. Its consequence is a significant worsening of the Triffin dilemma to the extent that net additions to reserves are invested mainly in US debt instruments, even though this trend has slowed down.

Addressing this complex problem requires a comprehensive set of measures. Indeed, a mere diversification of reserves could reduce the Triffin dilemma but would not eliminate the other negative aspects, while the enlarging of IMF financial facilities, even up to the level required by the LOLR function, could decrease somewhat the desire for reserve accumulation but probably not the preference for autonomous intervention policies. In such conditions, market reserves are likely to remain abundant and kept mostly in USD, with a still significant Triffin dilemma, unless a liquid private SDR market is developed, where public and private SDRs are linked. Thus, the solutions to be envisaged should be comprehensive and cover all aspects related to SDRs, both public and private.

4. The need for a stable reserve currency.

According to recent statistics, the dollar's share in foreign reserves amounts to 62 %, while the euro's is 24 %. Other currencies play a marginal role. The SDR represents about 4 % of total reserves.

If one considers the three functions to be taken into account when assessing the quality of a reserve currency, the USD has no equivalent in two of them: unit of account and medium of exchange. It is used in a large majority of international contracts for invoicing, trading and settling, and

---

[79] George M. von Furstenberg, article "SDR" in *The New Palgrave Dictionary of Money and Finance*, Macmillan, 1992.

the liquidity, depth and size of its main financial markets are unique. In current circumstances, as long as the renminbi (RMB) does not play a significant international role, only the euro (EUR) could be considered a possible substitute in these functions, but the comparison cannot go very far as EUR capital markets are much smaller and also still segmented by national boundaries. BIS statistics show that the USD is one side of 87 % of all the trades in foreign exchange, while for the EUR it is only 33 %.

By contrast, if one considers the third function, namely store of value, the USD's performance appears much less satisfactory. The dollar has depreciated almost continuously in terms of goods (the CPI has more than quadrupled in the last 40 years). It has also depreciated against currencies in general, in particular against the German currency (DEM and then EUR). The decline is impressive, as the purchasing power of a USD against this reference has been divided by 2.5 since 1970. Actually, the USD has followed a long declining trend over the last four decades and, in addition, has been subject to intense short term cyclical pressures, up and down, according to changes in international investors' expectations. Although supposed to be an anchor, the USD was, at least no less than other currencies, subject to the vagaries of the floating exchange rate regime.

In this respect, the SDR would have been a much better standard in terms of long-term value and short-term stability. True, it too has depreciated against the price of goods. But while, by construction, it depreciated against strong currencies, like the DEM (later the EUR) and the Yen, it appreciated against the dollar (from 1.00 at its creation to about 1.50 now). Also, by virtue of its valuation as a basket of currencies, it has been more stable than any of its components. Although it cannot be used as an intervention currency unless and until it develops an active private market, it would be perfectly satisfactory as a precautionary reserve.

5. The need for an effective management of global liquidity.

Global liquidity comprises both private international financing and central bank reserves. Today, except in very rare circumstances such as during the 2009 crisis, these matters are not subject to any collective decision-making and are influenced mainly by monetary conditions in leading countries and by international financial market conditions. In particular since the FED's, as any other national Central Bank's, monetary policy is legitimately and unavoidably oriented towards the internal needs of the U.S. economy, this generates significant external effects on global liquidity, which are incompatible with the preservation of world economic stability.

Indeed, national monetary policies in the big countries influence strongly private international financing, generating huge flows through international financial institutions and the shadow banking system. This means that one has to take into consideration how liquidity creation and credit extension in major economies – especially those with large financial systems – are driven by their central banks and transmitted to other economies through global integrated markets and exchange rate movements. Today, there is no international instrument to regulate these elements. This is particularly damaging as monetary policies, considered individually, can be perfectly designed for national purposes, and yet have strong negative effects on the rest of the world, through an international financial system left largely out of control.[80] The PRI report made several suggestions in this respect in its 4th section.

Central bank reserves include both reserve currencies, mainly USD, held in the form of market instruments, and IMF reserve positions and SDRs.

As total reserves can derive from current account surpluses or capital flows and as quotas cannot be adjusted easily, the only element of global liquidity that, in practice, can be subject to collective decision-making is SDR holdings. The development of permanent financing mechanisms, akin to a global LOLR, is necessary. SDRs constitute the natural IMF instrument for this purpose and should play a much larger financial role than today. Such an approach would have the additional advantage of providing, at least to some degree, an effective alternative to further precautionary reserve accumulation.

6. The SDR as the best instrument for a gradual reform of the IMS.

The SDR offers several well-known advantages as a multilateral standard.

As a reserve asset, it is the only existing instrument which can be issued without being a direct liability of any single economy; it is therefore the easiest and most rational channel for providing alternative reserves to central banks that plan to build them up for facing any future crisis, without implying larger deficits for issuers of national reserve currencies. Furthermore, it is the only existing monetary reserve, which can be issued

---

80   Private international financing can be extremely volatile: from 2007 to 2009, gross capital inflows worldwide fell from nearly 20 % of global GDP to less than 2 %, leading to a massive SDR issue in 2009. Such extreme fluctuations have critical effects on the functioning of the global economic and financial system and on macro-financial stability at country level.

on the basis of available international official procedures. Finally, it is the only one that is accepted by "conventional officials and central bankers" since it already has an agreed institutional existence firmly locked in the IMF system.

As a store of value, the SDR is by construction an international standard: as it is defined by definite quantities of the different constitutive currencies, a weakening currency loses weight in the basket, while a strengthening one gains weight.[81] The SDR also offers a clear advantage from the standpoint of short-run stability, to the extent that its composition is aligned with the relative economic weights of different countries. In this respect the addition of the RMB at the first possible opportunity and later on of other emerging countries' currencies is to be strongly recommended. If the RMB is still not ready to enter the basket at the next five-year review (due to take place in 2015), the IMF should confirm that it would do so as soon as certain objective conditions are satisfied.

As a unit of account, the SDR has the advantage of being by definition immune to the impact of floating exchange rates; as such it would contribute to reduce the volatility of valuation, in comparison with the use of any single currency. Less volatility of valuation means less necessity to hedge, less impact from financial expectations and, finally, greater market stability. Even though its use would probably increase transaction costs, at least at the start, it could be useful as the invoicing currency in international contracts, especially those related to commodities.

However, its negligible share in official reserves and the absence of any private market are handicaps. Indeed, the use of the SDR is currently limited to rare movements inside the official sector, for amounts that remain insignificant, though this does not preclude the accumulation of substantial precautionary balances in SDRs. This cannot be sufficient for a comprehensive reform of the IMS, which should also include the possibility to use the SDR directly in interventions. This would imply extensive private holdings of SDRs and a significant SDR private market. The following two sections make concrete suggestions aiming, firstly, at enhancing the role of official SDRs in the IMS, and, secondly, at developing private SDR transactions on a significant market.

---

[81]   This loss/gain of weight is however reversed when the basket is revised conformingly.

III. Enhancing the role of official SDRs

7. Use the SDR more actively in the official sector life.

While the IMF's Articles of Agreement[82] envisage that the SDR would become the principal reserve asset in the international monetary system, very little has been done to give the SDR a greater role in the life of international institutions.

In particular, it remains regrettable that the IMF still conducts its General Account in terms of member currencies. There would be significant benefits to the IMF in converting all its operations to an SDR basis: this would enable the IMF to present a comprehensible balance sheet to the world, simplify its own accounting, and make it clear that a quota enlargement does not have a real resource cost (which is an important consideration in terms of US Congressional politics).

Similarly, the SDR should be given more visibility in IMF documents, surveys and statements, and more broadly in the life of the official sector. Initiatives should also be taken to develop the use of the SDR as a reference by international institutions in their accounts (following the BIS' example), their publications, and as far as possible their operations.

8. International Lender of Last Resort.

The ability of the IMF to act as an international LOLR is urgently needed in crisis situations, in order to provide, for countries that fear a repeat of 1997, an alternative to self-insurance. In order to activate this, the international community, presumably represented by the IMF Council (or until then, by the International Monetary and Financial Committee), should be required to declare that a crisis situation exists. Such a vote should empower the IMF to issue unlimited quantities of SDRs (liabilities against itself) to be used in financing programmes for helping member countries in need.

9. General SDR allocations.

There is a major need to resume the practice of making general SDR allocations. The third general allocation, which was made on August 28th 2009, in the amount of SDR 161.2 bn[83], to cushion the effects of the

---

[82] Article XXII of the Articles of Agreement stipulates that "each participant undertakes to collaborate with the Fund and with other participants in order to facilitate the effective functioning of the Special Drawing Rights Department and the proper use of special drawing rights in accordance with this Agreement and with the objective of making the special drawing right the principal reserve asset in the international monetary system".

[83] Separately, the Fourth Amendment to the Articles of agreement became effective August 10, 2009 and provided for a special one-time allocation of SDR 21.5 bn to

financial crisis on global liquidity, was an example of what can be done, in case of need, at the global level. However, regular allocations should not follow a pre-defined programme, as laid out in the IMF Articles. Instead, the amount should be determined on an *ad hoc* basis[84], after a survey of liquidity conditions jointly conducted by the IMF and the BIS which, since October 2013, publishes updates on indicators for global liquidity conditions, together with the underlying BIS data.

10. Targeted allocations.

Restricting the creation of additional SDR liquidities to general allocations according to existing rules, that is in proportion to the quotas, would certainly miss the target since the main part of these new reserve would be allocated to countries which do not need them (the main quotas holders), while the majority of small and fragile countries would only obtain a marginal part of the allocation.

A possible solution proposed by the working party would be to allocate 20 % (say) to advanced countries and 80 % (say) to emerging markets and developing countries, with allocations within each group in proportion to IMF quotas. This solution would avoid the danger of losing the discipline imposed by limited reserve holding and maintain the principle that allocations should remain independent of national perception of need, while greatly mitigating the problem of misdistribution.

Some members propose, in addition, a more flexible approach, which would not retain quotas as the unique allocation criterion but rely also upon IMF expertise and adequate surveillance to allow the opening of SDR denominated financing mechanisms to individual countries in need of preventive reserves. They see this facility as an effective alternative to precautionary reserve accumulation. Establishing such new individual allocations would imply a specific attention by the Fund to necessary safeguards and to the liquidity of its SDR position.

In both cases, a revision of the Fund's Articles would be needed.

11. Diversification of reserves.

One could consider stand-by procedures, rule-based, through which central banks could acquire SDRs against currencies, upon request. The idea of a "substitution account" open permanently or on a periodic basis (for instance

---

members who had not benefited from previous allocations.

[84]   This means that, in the current circumstances, the SDR Working Party does not presuppose that new SDR issues would be needed.

twice a year for predetermined amounts) should be revived. Another possibility is to give the IMF the faculty to buy against SDRs currency reserves, for instance those coming in addition to the ones already built up by countries at a determined date. Selling the proportion of the acquired currency (say USD), necessary for the purchase by the IMF of the other part of the SDR basket (currently EUR, GBP and JPY), would influence markets, but less than if the full amount (of USD) were sold by the central bank in search of reserve diversification. This operation would generate no exchange risk for the IMF.

12. SDRs and the Triffin dilemma.

General SDR allocations made according to existing rules, in proportion of quotas, would be freed from any Triffin dilemma if quotas truly reflected the relative importance of member's economies; as this is not the case, the problem would not be entirely eliminated though considerably reduced. In other cases (targeted allocations, private SDRs), SDR issues would not solve the Triffin dilemma, but they would contribute to reduce its intensity and smooth its negative effects. In the case of reserve diversification, the Triffin dilemma would be at least mitigated through the fact that the "exorbitant privilege" would be spread across countries whose currencies make up the SDR basket, reducing the asymmetry of the dollar and introducing some external constraint on the US economy. For the non-dollar part of the SDR, the so-called "privilege" would be transferred from the dollar to other basket currencies, but the IMS would be improved by the fact that the system would no longer be based on the debt of a single country but of several countries, representing a much larger part of the world economy and trade. The better the basket would represent the composition of world GDP, the more the dilemma would be reduced.

13. Making the SDR more attractive and user-friendly.

Ways to make the SDR more appealing should be considered. Smoothing the administrative rules applicable when a country decides to use its SDRs would certainly be welcome. For example, the IMF could be put in the position to convert immediately, upon request, SDRs into usable currencies, either out of its own resources, by negotiating with the issuing national central bank, or by relying on private currency markets. Also, the way interest rates are calculated should also be revised, replacing the present short-term rates basis by medium- and longer-term references. If, as is envisaged, a private SDR market were to develop, the use of a market rate or a range of market rates would anyhow substitute the present administrative procedures for the remuneration of official SDR assets and liabilities.

Suggestion A: Give the SDR a greater international public role.

First of all, the IMF's accounts should be placed on an all-SDR basis, requiring an amalgamation of the General Resources Account with the SDR account and that future lending would all be in SDRs. International organizations that are not using the SDR as their unit of account should also be invited to do so, following the example of the BIS. In addition, the IMF and other international institutions should use the SDR more systematically as a reference in their work, in particular in the domains of international statistics, balance of payments, international reserves, article IV exercises, surveillance of exchange rates, capital flows analyses, etc. Also, international public contracts should, whenever possible, employ the SDR as an unit of account, and the use of the SDR in government borrowing should be encouraged; this would incite the private sector to do the same, for example in commodities contracts.

Suggestion B: The IMF should be enabled to issue SDRs at last resort in a crisis situation.

When the IMF Council (or, pending that, the International Monetary and Financial Committee) declares a crisis situation, the IMF should gain the power to issue SDRs to itself through an institutionalized mechanism, and to lend them to member countries affected by the crisis.

Suggestion C: The IMF should resume SDR allocations.

General allocations should be decided year by year on the basis of an assessment of global conditions, undertaken jointly by the IMF and the BIS.

However, restricting the creation of additional SDR liquidities to general allocations according to existing rules, that is, in proportion to the quotas, would result in allocating the main part of new reserves to the main quotas holders which generally do not need them, while the majority of small and fragile countries would only obtain a small part of the allocation. Two solutions could be envisaged:

One would be to mitigate the problem of misdistribution by allowing only a marginal part of the allocation to advanced countries and the main part of it to emerging markets and developing countries, with allocation within each group in proportion to IMF quotas. This solution would avoid the danger of losing the discipline imposed by limited reserve holding and would maintain the principle that allocations should remain independent of national perception of need.

Another solution, aiming at a more flexible approach and favoured by only some members of the working party, would not retain quotas as the unique allocation criterion but rely also upon IMF expertise, adequate surveillance and specific attention to the liquidity of the Fund's SDR position, to allow the opening of SDR-denominated financing mechanisms to individual countries in need of preventive reserves.

Both solutions would necessitate a revision of the Fund's Articles.

Suggestion D: An orderly diversification of reserves

Reserve diversification should be facilitated through a mechanism allowing their conversion into SDR-denominated claims. In particular, periodical substitution account facilities should be offered to member countries, and currency exchange operations against SDRs should be organized between the IMF and its members.

Suggestion E: SDRs should be made more attractive.

SDR interest rates should be based on medium or long term yields rather than short term, and rules applicable to the conversion of SDRs into marketable currencies should be simplified if possible, with the IMF acting as a financial intermediary temporarily until such operations can be carried out by private intermediaries in the market.

Suggestion F: The composition of the basket should reflect more closely the relative importance of economies in international trade and financial transactions.

In particular, the introduction of the RMB into the basket should be envisaged as soon as the internationalization of this currency will allow it.

IV. Promoting a private SDR market

14. The need for an SDR market.

The role of the SDR in central bank reserves would be greatly enhanced if these institutions could use the SDR as a market asset. To this end, the development of a private SDR market should be strongly encouraged to the point where its liquidity becomes significant. It is clear that, from a technical point of view, the development of an SDR market is much more the business of financial institutions than of the official sector. However, it is the responsibility of the latter to take the lead at the start. Indeed, for the time being, the financial sector appears to have little appetite for SDR instruments, even though it would probably react positively if significant demand was expressed by clients. In spite of this, there are financial instruments in the market that are akin to SDRs such as Currency-Basket

Exchange-Traded Funds (ETFs), which are attractive for institutional investors.[85] There might also be a potential interest on the part of non-financial corporations (e.g. for those engaged in commodity markets), but it is also unlikely that they are prepared to move spontaneously. Hence, the initiative should come from the public sector.

This initiative should be resolute as the aim should be to reach a critical mass sufficient to make SDR markets competitive with those for other internationally used currencies in terms of transaction costs, depth, liquidity and range of available financial products. Tradability of SDRs appears to be a first step in rendering them acceptable to private markets and thus giving them a greater role in private finance. Reaching this critical mass could require a significant degree of public policy action, which might be justified by "infant market" considerations. Re-creating a private SDR market more than thirty years after the few operations, which existed in the past, vanished would thus necessitate big efforts on the part of public authorities and their close cooperation with market participants. Indeed, whatever steps are taken by the public sector to create a good environment favourable to the emergence of a significant SDR financial market, there would be little chance of success if market operators were not convinced of the robustness of this initiative, in terms of costs/advantages for their clients and for themselves. Hence, appropriate structures should be put in place to ensure the adequate coordination between market specialists of the official and the private sectors.

15. The need for SDR Clearing arrangements.

As soon as a number of banks start offering SDR bank deposits, some form of interbank SDR market will need to come into existence. The more efficient way to clear bilateral interbank transactions would be to create a multilateral clearing, at least among a number of high quality participants, on the model of the former ECU clearing operated in the past by the BIS. Setting up such clearing arrangements either through an existing international institution or through a specific private body to be created is a necessary condition to the development of a private SDR market, and it would be needed from the start.[86]

---

[85] However the market tends to create various ETFs whose composition is tailored to the needs of financial investors, which does not necessarily match the composition of an official SDR basket. However a passive ETF (basket of currencies) with pass-through or neutral currency board arrangements could also be of interest to investors, in particular State Pension Funds and Sovereign Wealth Funds.

[86] Initially this could be facilitated by allowing a small number of selected banks, say the 10 most active in currency markets, to trade a marketable SDR not on the exchanges,

16. Providing legal certainty and practicable administrative rules.

The development of markets in SDR financial instruments requires legal certainty and continuity regarding the content of this unit. The periodical basket revisions could be a source of uncertainty regarding the future properties of the basket, which depend on both present and future weights. One way to solve this potential problem would be to make the introduction of the RMB in the basket as soon as it is possible (see suggestion F), to pre-announce the times of future basket revisions, and to implement transparent rules regarding the variables and the data to be used in re-calculating the weights, so that market participants could form reasonable forecasts of each revision's outcome.

17. Developing private SDR operations by the public sector.

Several initiatives could be envisaged:

- In order to provide a critical mass to the development of an SDR debt market, major international institutions active in bond markets as regular issuers should start issuing SDR-denominated bonds. This could well be a triggering point as central banks might be interested in holding these financial assets, even before the development of mature SDR financial markets.

  Using the possibilities offered by the Articles of Agreement, the IMF itself could also, as far as needed, issue long term SDR bonds that would be floated on a regular basis and which central banks could subscribe to in parallel to private investors. The flotation of these SDR denominated bonds would be a good diversification instrument for central banks, and the possibility to trade them with private financial institutions would contribute to the development of the market.

  Owing to the occurrence of basket revisions, short-term instruments are expected to have a better chance to succeed at first. However, if SDR markets are to develop, there will quickly be a need to offer an SDR yield curve with a sufficient array of maturities.

- While governments are well-advised to issue debt in their own currencies, there would be room for them to issue some in SDRs. National public entities could also use the SDR for invoicing and possibly settling their contracts with foreign entities and could

---

but through official Real-Time-Gross-Settlement Systems (RTGS) of central banks as executed by the private CLS bank currently.

encourage doing the same in private international contracts, in particular for commodities.

- If the SDR became a significant component of central bank foreign reserves and if an active "private" SDR market were to take shape, swap operations could be needed in order to strengthen the liquidity of this developing market and to facilitate SDR use.

18. Linking private and official SDRs.

In order to enable central banks to use their official SDR holdings directly on private markets, it is necessary to create a link between private and official SDRs. This could be achieved either by allowing private banks to hold SDRs or by allowing the official SDRs to be converted into claims that central banks and private banks could hold.

Allowing private banks and institutions to hold SDRs on the Fund's book would be a major positive step, even though it would necessitate a change in the Fund's Articles.

Alternatively, the link between official and private SDRs could be built upon the interbank clearing arrangements described in §15. Central banks could get private SDRs by establishing deposits with the clearinghouse and transferring to its name official SDRs. If the clearinghouse is already a "prescribed holder" of SDRs, this procedure would be easy to put in place; if it is a private sector institution, a procedure of agreement would be needed.

However beyond this institutional aspect the clearing house would be confronted with specific risks linked to the fact that it would have to load on one side of its balance sheet official SDRs underpinned by the financial activities of the IMF and, on the other side, private SDRs bearing different credit-related characteristics attached to the issuer's credit (a government, a financial institution, or even a corporate...). This risk mismatch, inherent to bank activities but less compatible with a clearing function, could become a major impediment when the market develops unless the clearinghouse gets from its members appropriate guaranties. These matters merit discussions with market specialists.

Suggestion G: The official sector should take the lead in providing appropriate structures suited to the functioning of an active SDR market.

It should first ensure a proper degree of legal certainty, especially in the domain of basket revisions, and reassess the conditions in which the forex rate fixing is organized. It should also facilitate the establishment of appropriate clearing arrangements.

Suggestion H: Subject to necessary adjustment to existing statutory rules, international institutions and national authorities should start operating in private SDRs.

In order to provide a critical mass to the development of an SDR debt market, SDR – denominated debt instruments should be floated by international institutions, first and foremost the World Bank and other supranational IFIs, and on a limited scale by national authorities. The latter should also consider invoicing international public contracts in SDR, and encourage the use of the SDR in private international contracts, in particular for commodities.

Suggestion I: The IMF should name a limited number of leading private banks as holders of SDRs.

This would have the effect of linking the circuits of official and private SDRs but would necessitate an amendment to the Fund's articles.

In conclusion, the Working Party is convinced that the first best solution to solve the weaknesses inherent to the present International Monetary System would be to create a multilateral currency, with the IMF acting as a central bank and national central banks holding all their reserves as claims on the IMF. However it admits that such a fundamental change is not likely in the current geopolitical environment and, in making the best of the existing system, it sees the SDR as the best available option to improve the IMS. With a minimum of political will, a lot could already be done in the domains of official and private SDRs, without having to adjust the IMF's Articles of Agreement. However, for the reform to be significant, a private SDR market should be strongly encouraged and for this it is necessary that a link be institutionalized between official and private SDRs with a view to allowing central banks to use their official SDRs directly in intervention. For these purposes, a limited number of amendments to the IMF's Articles of Agreement are necessary.

****

Appendix
Composition of the SDR Working Party(*)

Hervé Carré	Former Director General, European Commission
Elena Flor	Corporate Social Responsibility Manager, Intesa Sanpaolo Group
Christian Ghymers	Former Adviser, European Commission; Deputy Secretary General, Triffin International Foundation

André Icard	Former Deputy General Manager of the Bank for International Settlements; Chairman of the Working Party
Alfonso Iozzo	Former Managing Director, San Paolo IMI; Vice President, Triffin International Foundation
Jean-Claude Koeune	Emeritus Professor, *Université Catholique de Louvain* Secretary General, Triffin International Foundation
Antonio Mosconi	President, *Centro Einstein di Studi Internazionali*
Andrew Sheng	President, Fung Global Institute, Hong Kong
Paul Bernd Spahn	Emeritus Professor of Economics, Goethe-Universität, Frankfurt-am-Main
John Williamson	Senior Fellow (retired), Peterson Institute for International Economics

Experts consulted at the Paris meeting on 18 December 2013

Denis Beau	Director General of Operations at *Banque de France*
Dominique Hoenn	Senior Advisor and former Co-Chief Operating Officer at BNP Paribas
Günter Pleines	Former Head of the Banking Department at BIS
Xin Wang	Chief Representative, Repr. Office in Frankfurt, The People's Bank of China.

(*) The Working Party held three meetings: in Brussels on 10 October 2013, in Paris on 18-19 December 2013, in Brussels on 8 May 2014.

C. The Robert Triffin International

Robert Triffin International (RTI), was created just a few years after Triffin's death, on the initiative of Alexander Lamfalussy and with the support of Compagnia di San Paolo. It was the first to assemble – in collaboration with the National Bank of Belgium (Research Department) and the University of Luxembourg (Centre Pierre Werner) – Triffin's papers on his work at the US Treasury, the Fed, the IMF, the EPU alongside his scholarly works: first at Yale, then at the Catholic University of Louvain-la-Neuve. His books, articles, reports, memoranda, letters have now been collected, catalogued and made available at the University Centre for the History of Contemporary Europe. I addition, RTI has promoted research and publications on Triffin's life and work and has furthered his efforts towards reforming the international monetary system during the critical transition from a hegemonic to a multi-polar system.

RTI brings together more than fifty figures who have played significant roles in Europe and worldwide. Many members were Professor Triffin's students in the US or Belgium. RTI is known throughout the world (in particular in the US, the EU, Latin America and China) for its research and proposals aimed at overcoming the inherent instability in the use of national currencies as international currency. Robert Triffin's ideas have inspired personalities such as Zhou Xiaochuan, Governor of the People's Bank of China; Raghuram Rajan, who was Governor of the Reserve Bank of India; and José Antonio Ocampo,[87] former Deputy Secretary General of the UN. Moreover, RTI played a part in helping the IMF evolve into a more multilateral framework, characterised by the greater weight of emerging economies, a multi-currency reserve system and the greater role of the SDR.

In November 2009, encouraged by the results of the G20, Alexandre Lamfalussy promoted "Initiative Triffin 21" with the aim of contributing to the debate on the reform of the international monetary system, drawing on Triffin's proposals and adapting them for the 21st century. The first step in this initiative was a lecture by Tommaso Padoa-Schioppa, given at the

---

[87] José Antonio Ocampo (1952) is a Professor of Professional Practice in International and Public Affairs and Director of economics and development policy in Colombia. He has held important positions in the United Nations (Under Secretary General for Economic and Social Affairs, Executive Secretary of the Economic Commission for Latin America and the Caribbean), in his own country (Minister of Finance and Minister of Agriculture) and in the academic world (Executive Director of Fedesarrollo, Director of the Centre for Studies on Economic Development, a Professor of Economics at the University of Los Andes, a Professor of Economic History at the National Colombia University). He is the author of a number of books and essays.

Catholic University of Louvain-la-Neuve (UCL) on 25 February 2010 entitled *The Ghost of Bancor: The economic Crisis and Global Monetary Disorder.*[88] Padoa-Schioppa expressed his ideas so effectively, clearly and elegantly that we would like to quote a few passages below.

The deep causes of this crisis include the dollar policy and, in a broader sense, the monetary regime that has been in force in the world for almost 40 years. Like the Bretton Woods system, it is incapable of imparting an acceptable macroeconomic discipline to the world's economy because, being devoid of collectively accepted anchors, it encourages the persistence of unsustainable dynamics which spawn increasingly serious crises. Triffin's criticism of an international monetary system based on an exclusively national monetary policy is still valid, although today it demands a broader formulation, capable of taking into account the exchange rate anarchy and a multiplicity of influential monetary policies. The issue of international monetary order is not being afforded due attention and it needs to be addressed [...]

Globalization is indeed what allowed American families to buy manufactured goods and services at prices determined not by their own salaries but by the far lower salaries of Asian workers or Indian computer programmers. Thus the economies' open nature had a crucial impact also on the domestic aspect, due to the paralysis of the domestic monetary policy indicators in the country issuing the international currency [...]

Two crucial factors made it possible to protract this navigation far beyond the point at which a route adjustment could still have been painless: the fact that it was the world's leading economic power sailing that route; and the fact that that economy, being the world's central banker, was exempted from any external monetary discipline [...]

Economic interdependence is a fact. The sovereignty which governments consider to be inalienable is no longer absolute, because it has been removed by economic interdependence itself rather than by any specific monetary regime. There is no monetary regime capable of rebuilding it while maintaining the benefits of interdependence. The foreign exchange market is incapable either of eliminating or of governing interdependence because it is too slow in detecting the imbalances that require correction, and when it does detect them, it is incapable of enforcing decisions on the public players who are responsible for those imbalances" [...] What we might call Triffin's 'general

---

[88] The text is available in English and French, on the RTI website: www.triffininternational. eu. Moreover it was published in the author's recent collection of essays, edited by Antonio Padoa Schioppa and Carlo Maria Fenu: Tommaso Padoa-Schioppa, *The Ghost of Bancor. Essays on the Crisis, Europe and the Global Monetary Order*, Bologna, 2016, from which quotes have been taken and translated (p. 59, p. 65, pp. 76-77, p. 78, p. 85, pp. 85-86, pp. 88-89).

dilemma' can thus be expressed as follows: the stability requirements of the system as a whole are inconsistent with the pursuit of economic and monetary policy forged solely on the basis of domestic rationales in all monetary regimes devoid of some form of supranationality [...]

Regional monetary arrangements could facilitate the path toward reconstruction. If the exchange rate system has to be consistent with the degree of integration of the economy to which it applies, then we cannot overlook the fact that the globalization process is to a great extent a galaxy of regional integration processes. It is more than likely that vast regions with strong local interdependence will move toward regional monetary arrangements comparable to those which Europe sought when the Bretton Woods system came to an end. East Asia appears to be heading in that direction [...]

In the past, the number of currencies (n) exceeded the number of countries by one. The so-called n-th currency, the ultimate standard, was gold, the scarcity of which could not be countered by any national bank bill printing press. Could a man-made standard fulfil at least some of the functions of a global currency? Interest in this question has revived in the aftermath of the crisis and attention has naturally turned to the Special Drawing Right (SDR). Obviously, the condition *sine qua non* for SDR's to play a greater role in the international monetary system and to become a global standard is that they be able to circulate in the economy, that they be used by a broad spectrum of public and private economic players [...]

All of this is possible and offers a number of benefits, but the crucial question is this: would an SDR endowed with a well-developed private market, and used as a store of value and unit of account by private and public players, help to correct the fundamental flaw in the present system? My answer is positive, but sobering: yes it would, but only to the extent to which the average is better than the dominant component; beyond that limit, a global standard requires its 'own' policymaker mandated to pursue the global interest if it is to become a fully-fledged anchor of stability". [Here Padoa-Schioppa refers to the fact that the SDR is an *ecu-like* currency and not yet a *euro-like* one].

On 14 May 2010, Tommaso Padoa-Schioppa, along with Lamfalussy, presided over an international colloquium on *Initiative Triffin 21: Towards a world reserve currency*, organised by RTI, which brought together politicians, central bankers and economists from all over the world in Turin, united by their desire to develop a multilateral approach to international economic and monetary problems. The colloquium focused on two preliminary aspects of each reform proposal: 1) analysing the unsustainability of the current international monetary "non-system", a permanent source of instability and crisis, and 2) defining the requirements of a stable international monetary system.

Padoa-Schioppa became further involved by giving to the initiative his great intellect and professional skills, as well as the international reputation hence earned. Moreover, he promoted, along with Lamfalussy and Michel Camdessus,[89] the *Palais Royal Initiative*. This group of eighteen experts from thirteen countries (former ministers, central bank governors and representatives of national and international institutions) met several times in late 2010 and early 2011 at the *Palais Royal* in Paris, now the headquarters of the Banque de France. In February the group submitted a report, the *Palais Royal Initiative – Reform of the International Monetary System: A Cooperative Approach for the 21st Century*,[90] as a contribution to the G20 finance ministers' meeting that was held that same month. In January a summary of it was sent to the French Presidency of the G20.

The report – dedicated to the memory of Padoa-Schioppa,[91] who sadly passed away unexpectedly on 18 December 2010 – notes that, even after the crisis and re-regulation measures adopted by many countries, there are still serious threats to the stability of the international monetary system. These demand that governments pay urgent attention: the absence of a regulation driving the system towards rebalancing, meaning that deep reforms of multilateral surveillance of national policies is needed; exchange rate behavior must be brought in line with the needs of ordered adjustment and efficient allocation of resources; difficulties in the management of global liquidity must be prevented from causing avoidable inflation and deflation; the role of the SDR must be defined; governance issues, which are implicit in the decision-making processes, must be defined and resolved. To achieve these

---

[89] Michel Camdessus (1933), a former student of the ENA, had worked for the Treasury since 1960, of which he was appointed Director in 1982. From 1984 to 1987 he was Governor of the Banque de France – of which he remained the Honorary Governor – and from 1987 to 2000 he was Director of the IMF. In the thirteen difficult years that he led the Fund, he has addressed financial imbalances by trying to reconcile orthodoxy with solidarity. He assisted the economic transition of former Soviet countries, cancelled the poorest countries' debts, and tried to prevent crises or at least to make their outcomes less painful.

[90] The report was published in a volume that also collected documents prepared for preliminary discussions, contributions of the participants in the Initiative and contributions of other experts:

Jack T. Boorman and André Icard (eds.), *Reform of the International Monetary System. The Palais Royal Initiative*, New Delhi, 2011.

[91] *Ibid.*: "with him, the world has lost an eminent architect and advocate of the global common good."

results, the report provided eighteen specific recommendations, three of which concern: the extension of the role of the SDR as a reserve asset, unit of account and financial market instrument; an increasingly representative and realistic composition of the SDR basket (the inclusion of the renminbi was still *sub judice*); the strengthening of the IMF's authority by possibly linking it to the allocation of SDRs to comply with established standards and objectives for a more effective multilateral surveillance system.

In 2013 RTI set up – with Michel Camdessus's encouragement and participation – a working group, made up of its members and chaired by André Icard.[92] According to this group's work, published in 2014, the SDR would be a lever for the reform of the international monetary system.[93]

In short, the report, starting with the conclusions of the *Palais Royal Initiative* and more closely examining its suggestions,

- confirms that the current international monetary system has a built-in destabiliser, caused by using national currencies (especially the US dollar) as the international currency;
- recalls how *the nth* currency, independent of the (n-1) countries participating in the system, is the best theoretical solution, but considers that (from a political point of view) this objective cannot be achieved for a long time and suggests that the SDR is the second-best solution to launch the reform of the international monetary system;
- acknowledges the major limitations to the greater use of the SDR: its modest participation in the formation of reserves and the absence of an SDR-denominated market in financial instruments;
- proposes in consequence a series of actions to develop the official role of the SDR and promote a market in SDR-denominated financial instruments;
- with regard to the official role of the SDR, recalls how little has been done to achieve the objective set out in the IMF's Articles of Agreement, that the SDR become the system's main reserve currency, and offers six suggestions:

---

[92]　André Icard (1941), from 1964 to 1995 held positions of responsibility at the Banque de France in the areas of Surveillance, Balance of payments, Foreign exchange, Financial markets (when it participated in the modernisation of Paris' money and financial market) and General Manager of the economic department. He was then Deputy General Manager of the Bank for International Settlements (1996-2005).

[93]　Triffin International Foundation, "Using the Special Drawing Rights as a Lever to Reform the International Monetary System" – see Annex 2.

1) expand the SDR's public role by systematically using it in the IMF's financial transactions, promoting its use as a unit of account by international institutions (as the BIS already does), in international statistical measurements, public contracts and government issues;

2) give the IMF the power to issue SDRs upon providing an emergency statement from the international community, without a quantitative limit;

3) resume general periodic allocations of SDRs based on assessments of the state of international liquidity;

4) allow for the ordered diversification of reserves by replacing national currencies with SDRs;

5) improve the attractiveness of investment in SDRs in terms of returns;

6) bring the SDR basket in line with the relative importance of the economies, first of all, by including the RMB (achieved in 2016);

– offers three recommendations for forming a market:

1) that the public sector create the necessary structural conditions for the functioning of a market, namely clear, simple legislation that is both legal and operational, especially with regard to basket reviews, the adjustment of the exchange market organisation and facilitation in setting up a multilateral clearing system (modelled on the one already managed by the BIS for the ECU market);

2) that international institutions and national authorities issue SDR-denominated debt to give critical mass to the formation of a market, and that national authorities consider the second billing of international public contracts in SDRs and encourage the use of SDRs by private individuals, in particular for raw materials;

3) that the IMF appoint a small number of major banks as agents in the SDR market, so as to connect official and market SDR circuits.

Most of these recommendations do not require amendments to the Articles of the Fund, but to make the reform truly effective the official circuit must be effectively linked to the market circuit, so that central banks can directly use SDRs in their interventions. To that end, limited amendments to the articles are necessary.

A paper entitled *The International Monetary System, 70 Years after Bretton Woods: The Role of the Special Drawing Rights* was presented in November 2014 at the Lingotto in Turin during an international conference, organised by RTI and the Agnelli Foundation to foster an informal communication channel between managers and scholars, public and private players, including players from China.

Padoa-Schioppa was commemorated on that occasion in the speeches of John Elkann[94] ("In Memory of Tommaso Padoa-Schioppa") and Fabrizio Saccomanni[95] ("Tommaso Padoa-Schioppa and the Problem of Stability of the World Monetary Order").

The meeting in Turin was focused on the renminbi, with speeches by Chinese speakers Ping Sun[96] and Qiao Yide[97] to show how adding the renminbi to the basket would increase SDR representativeness as well as international monetary stability, and how the IMF's conditions had already been achieved since convertibility is not a requirement and the IMF Board's decision requires no other parliamentary procedures.

Along with the Shanghai Development Research Foundation (SDRF), the Reinventing Bretton Woods Committee (RBWC), the PBC School of Finance at Tsinghua University and the Shanghai Advanced Institute of Finance of Shanghai Jiao Tong University, RTI subsequently helped organise the seminar Shift in Global Financial Governance, held in Shanghai in November 2015 on the eve of the SDR basket review, during which President Bernard Snoy[98] explained RTI's work, with particular reference to the SDR and the inclusion of the renminbi in the basket.

---

[94]   John Elkann (1976), President and CEO of Exor, President of FCA Group. See: John Elkann, "In Memory of Tommaso Padoa-Schioppa", in *The Federalist Debate*, No. 1, March 2015.

[95]   Fabrizio Saccomanni (1942) joined the Bank of Italy in 1967, serving as general manager from 2006 to 2013. He was Minister of Economy and Finance (2013-2014) and is a member of the BIS Board of Directors and Deputy Governor in the ECB's Governing Council. He has actively participated in RTI's main initiatives.

[96]   Ping Sun, China's Alternate Director for the IMF.

[97]   Yide Qiao is Vice President and Secretary General of the Shanghai Development Research Foundation, Shanghai.

       Qiao Yide and Jiafei Ge, "Adding the RMB into the SDR basket: An Evaluation", in *The Federalist Debate*, No. 1, March 2015.

[98]   Baron Bernard Snoy et d'Oppuers (1945) worked at the World Bank from 1974 to 1979 (first West Africa, then Europe Middle East and North Africa); was Assistant Director of Kredietbank (1979-1980), then again of the World Bank in charge of financial relations at the European headquarters in Paris (1980-1986); economic adviser to the Directorate General for Economic and Financial Affairs at the Commission in Brussels (1986-1988); Head of Cabinet of the Belgian Minister of Finance (1988-1991); then Executive Director of the World Bank (1991-1994); Director of the European Bank for Reconstruction and Development in London, representing Belgium, Luxembourg and Slovenia (1994-2002); Director for economic reconstruction, development and cooperation in the Stability Pact for South Eastern Europe in Brussels (2002-2005); Coordinator of the OSCE's Economic and Environmental Activities in Vienna (2005-2008). Since 2008 he has been a visiting professor at UCL's Institute of European Studies. In 2013 he replaced Lamfalussy as President of RTI.

Bibliography

ATTALI, Jacques, *Un homme d'influence. Sir Siegmund Warburg 1902-1982*, Paris, Fayard, 1985.

Atti del Convegno (Proceedings of the Conference), "Un mercato finanziario italiano in euroscudi", Trieste, 21 March 1981, in *Quaderni dell'Istituto per gli Studi Assicurativi*, No. 34.

BORIO, Claudio, "More Pluralism, More Stability?", presentation at the Seventh High-level SNB-IMF Conference on the International Monetary System, May 2016.

BUTI, Marco, "The New Global Economic Governance. Can Europe Help Win the Peace?", *RTI-CSF Research Paper* (prepared as follow up of the Triffin Lecture given in Brussels, on 6 June 2017), Turin/Louvain-la-Neuve, July 2017.

CAMPANELLA, Miriam, "The Internazionalization of the Renminbi and the Rise of a Multipolar Currency System", *ECIPE Working Paper*, No. 01/2014.

COHEN, Benjamin J., "Should China Be Ejected from the SDR?", in *Project Syndicate*, 30 May 2017.

Commission of the European Communities, "The units of account as a factor of integration", Information Directorate-General – Economy and Finance, No 87/1975.

DESIATA, Alfonso, "L'Euroscudo nei rapporti assicurativi", in *Bancaria*, 1981.

European Commission, "Reflection Paper on the Deepening of the Economic and Monetary Union", Brussels, 31 May 2017.

FERRANT, Catherine and SLOOVER, Jean (Eds.), *Robert Triffin, Conseiller de princes. Souvenirs et documents*, Bruxelles, Peter Lang, 2010.

FLOR, Elena, "Un barile senza dollaro. Greggio, grano, monete: quanto pesa la speculazione", in *Il Sole 24 Ore*, 7 June 2017.

HAMMES, David and DOUGLAS, Wills, "Black Gold. The End of Bretton Woods and the Oil-Price Shocks of the 1970s", in *The Independent Review*, Vol. IX, No. 4, Spring 2005.

HARROD, Roy Forbes, *The Life of John Maynard Keynes*, London, Macmillan, 1951.

HOGUET, George and TADESSE, Solomon, "The Role of SDR-Denominated Securities in Official and Private Portfolios", in *BIS Paper*, No. 58, 2011.

IMF, "The Role of the SDR Initial Considerations", Staff Notes for the G20, Washington, 15 July 2016.

Iozzo, Alfonso, "From the ECU to the SDR", introduction to the paper by Tosolini, Valentina, "The ECU and the SDR: Learning from the Past, Preparing the Future", *RTI-CSF Research Paper*, Turin/Louvain-la-Neuve, November 2014.

Iozzo, Alfonso, "Luigi Arcuti, un banchiere per l'Europa", in *Il Sole 24 Ore*, 19 January 2013.

Jurgensen, Philippe, *ECU. Naissance d'une monnaie*, Paris, J.C. Lattès, 1991.

Keynes, John Maynard, *The Economic Consequences of the Peace*, New York, Harcourt, Brace and Howe, 1920.

Keynes, John Maynard, *The General Theory of Employment, Interest and Money*, London, Macmillan, 1936.

Lagarde, Christine, "Central Banking and Fintech – A Brave New World?", Bank of England Conference, London, 29 September 2017 (available at: https://www.imf.org/en/News/Articles/2017/09/28/sp092917-central-banking-and-fintech-a-brave-new-world).

Maes, Ivo and Pasotti, Ilaria, "The European Payments Union and the origins of Triffin's regional approach towards international monetary integration", Working Paper Research, National Bank of Belgium, September 2016, No. 301.

Magnifico, Giovanni, "L'unità di conto europea: considerazioni introduttive", in *Moneta e Credito*, 1976.

Makin, John H., "Swaps and Roosa Bonds as an Index of the Cost of Cooperation in the 'Crisis Zone'", in *The Quarterly Journal of Economics*, Harvard University's Department of Economics, May 1971.

Padoa-Schioppa, Tommaso, *La moneta e il sistema dei pagamenti*, il Mulino, Bologna, 1992.

Prometeia, *Forecast Report*, Bologna, March 2017.

Research and Treasurer's Departments IMF, *The Role of the SDR in the International Monetary System*, (edited by Roushdy, Juanita), IMF Occasional Paper, No. 51, March 1987.

Schumpeter, Joseph Alois, *History of Economic Analysis*, London, Allen & Unwin, 1954.

Skidelsky, Robert, *John Maynard Keynes. Fighting for Freedom, 1937-1946*, New York, Viking, 2000.

Sobol, Dorothy, "The SDR in International Private Finance", in *FRBNY Quarterly Review*, Winter 1981/82.

Steil, Benn, *The Battle of Bretton Woods. John Maynard Keynes, Harry Dexter White, and the Making of a New World Order*, Princeton University Press, 2013.

Tosolini, Valentina, "Analysing Commodity Prices: Trend for Crude Oil and Wheat in US Dollars, Euro and SDR", *RTI-CSF Research Paper*, Turin/Louvain-la-Neuve, December 2016.

TRIFFIN, Robert, *Our International Monetary System: Yesterday, Today and Tomorrow*, New York, Random House, 1968.

TRIFFIN, Robert *et al.*, "Verso una moneta europea" ("Towards a European Currency"), proceedings of the conference "For a European Reserve Monetary System" (Turin, 20 June 1970), in *Collana lo Spettatore Internazionale*, 1970.

TRIFFIN, Robert, *Dollaro, Euro e moneta mondiale*, edited by Iozzo, Alfonso and Steinherr, Alfred, Bologna, Il Mulino, 1998.

WILKIE, Christopher, *Special Drawing Rights. The First International Money*, Oxford University Press, New York, 2012.

WILSON, Jérôme, *Robert Triffin – Milieux académiques et cénacles économiques et internationaux (1935-1951)*, Bruxelles, Éditions Versant Sud, 2015.

ZHOU, Xiaochuang, "Reform the international monetary system", in *BIS Review*, 41/2009.

Federalism

The book series Federalism, run by the Centro Studi sul Federalismo/ Centre for Studies on Federalism (CSF) aims to disseminate knowledge in the field of studies on federalism, as well as to feed the academic and public debate and support the activity of decision-makers, confronted with demands for autonomy by local governments, along with forms of regional and world integration needed to govern global processes.

The book series is divided into two sub-series: Studies and Classics. The former mostly contains the research outcome and the proceedings of conferences and seminars promoted by the Centre, while the latter consists in reprints of the federalist classic works and English translations of Italian federalists' works.

The CSF is a think tank that carries out activities of interdisciplinary research, documentation, information regarding domestic and supranational federalism, developments in the area of regional and continental integration – first and foremost the European Union – and problems related to the world order and the process of democratisation of the international system. The CSF has been founded under the auspices of the Compagnia di San Paolo and the Universities of Turin, Pavia and Milan.

Centro Studi sul Federalismo
Piazza Vincenzo Arbarello 8
10122 Torino – Italy
Tel. + 39 011.6705024 Fax + 39 011.6705081
E-mail: info@csfederalismo.it
Website: www.csfederalismo.it

Series Editor: Lucio Levi, Former Professor of Political Science and Comparative Politics at the Turin University, Editor of The Federalist Debate and Scientific Director of the International Democracy Watch

Editorial Board

Series titles

No.1 – Giovanni Finizio and Ernesto Gallo (eds.), *Democracy at the United Nations. UN Reform in the Age of Globalisation*, 2012.

No.2 – Roberto Castaldi (ed.), *Immanuel Kant and Alexander Hamilton, the Founders of Federalism. A Political Theory for Our Time*, 2013.

No.3 – Claudio Giulio Anta (ed.), *Lord Lothian: The Paths of Federalism. Writings and Speeches*, 2014.

No.4 – Filippo Maria Giordano and Stefano dell'Acqua (eds.), *"Die Welt war meine Gemeinde". Willem A. Visser 't Hoof – A Theologian for Europe between Ecumenism and Federalism*, 2014.

No.5 – Giampiero Bordino (ed.), *A New Right for Democracy and Development in Europe. The European Citizens' Initiative (ECI)*, 2015.

No.6 – Filippo Maria Giordano, *Unity through Diversity. An Insight into Federalism and Ecumenism within Italian Protestantism*, 2016.

No.7 – Lucio Levi, Giampiero Bordino and Antonio Mosconi (eds.), *Federalism. A Political Theory for Our Time*, 2016.

No.8 – Lorenzo Vai, Pier Domenico Tortola and Nicoletta Pirozzi (eds.), *Governing Europe. How to Make the EU More Efficient and Democratic*, 2017.

No.9 – Korwa G. Adar, Giovanni Finizio and Angela Meyer (eds.), *Building Regionalism from Below. The Role of Parliaments and Civil Society in Regional Integration in Africa*, 2017.

No.10 – Alberto Majocchi, *European budget and sustainable growth. The Role of a Carbon Tax*, 2018.

No. 11 – Elena Flor, *SDR: from Bretton Woods to a world currency*, 2019.

www.peterlang.com